SESQUICENTENNIAL EXPOSITION
1776 UNITED STATES POSTAGE 1926
2 TWO CENTS 2
PHILLY
Daily Post
NO, TO BRITISH RULES IN THE COLONIES!
CHARLESTON

MY COLONY IS MY COUNTRY!
NEW YORK STATE U.S.
of the STAMP
An Emblem of the Effects
O! the fatal Stamp
NO TAXATION WITHOUT REPRESENTATION!
BOSTON TEA PARTY

FACTOLOGY
AMERICAN REVOLUTION

Open up a world of information!

REBELS WITH A CAUSE

Two hundred and fifty years after it happened, it's time to revisit a revolution. This incredible story begins with 13 overlooked colonies under careless British rule banding together to fight for their rights and claim independence. And they didn't stop there...

Within three decades these plucky outsiders had built a country that would become the most powerful nation on the planet. So, join the American revolutionaries on an epic journey through monumental events that would shape the lives of millions for generations to come.

CHAPTER 1
ROAD TO REVOLUTION

CHAPTER 2
IT'S WAR!

CHAPTER 3
WE THE PEOPLE

DUTCH TEA
BOSTON TEA PARTY
NO TAXATION WITHOUT REPRESENTATION!

CHAPTER 1

THE ROAD TO REVOLUTION

Why previously loyal British subjects decided to take control of their country.

WHAT WAS THE AMERICAN REVOLUTION?

King George III

- **During the American Revolution colonists freed themselves from the rule of Britain's King George III after winning the War of Independence (1775–1783).**
- It marked the beginning of the country we now know as the United States of America and had an impact throughout the rest of the world.
- The revolution led to the establishment of a country with its own laws, political system and president that was **free of rulers and tyranny**.
- This was all inspired by new ideas on what it meant to be a **citizen**.
- The American War of Independence was the first war fought over **human rights**.

The revolution brought together 13 self-governing colonies led by the Founding Fathers, men who promoted loyalty to God and country, and were inspired by the idea that people are created equal.

These leaders put in place a system that allowed their country to be governed by politicians on behalf of its people. And it included safeguards that protected the country from falling into the hands of one all-powerful ruler.

Before the revolution almost everyone on Earth lived under the rule of somebody else. This is why the revolution is seen as one of the most important events in history.

The 13 American colonies were all on the Atlantic coast

However...

The revolution was not just won by a small group of politicians. Millions of men, women and children made sacrifices for their colonies' victory but not all of them benefited from the changes made afterwards.

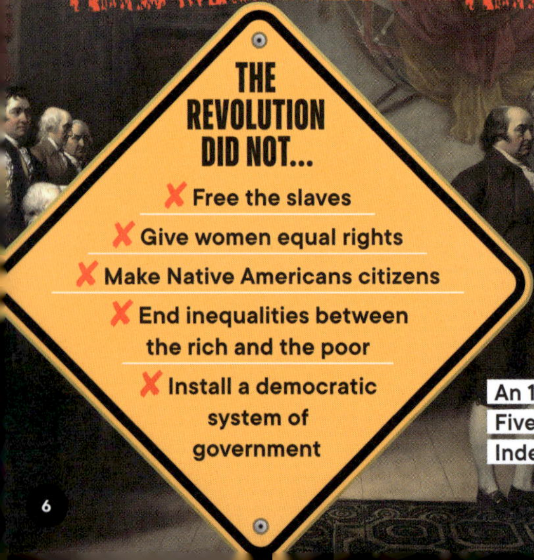

An 1818 painting of the 'Committee of Five' presenting the Declaration of Independence to Congress

An inspiration

The revolution established the United States as a country which looked to champion the freedom of the individual. In the centuries since, it has helped inspire people fighting for equal rights and fair treatment from their governments.

REVOLUTIONARY ROAD

1492 Christopher Columbus and his crew are the first European explorers to set foot in what would later be called the Americas.

1565 The Spanish establish the first European settlement in what is now the United States, at St Augustine, Florida.

1607 The first permanent British colony is established in Jamestown, Virginia.

1765

The British Parliament passes the Stamp Act and the Quartering Act.

1770 British troops open fire on a protest and kill five colonists in the Boston Massacre.

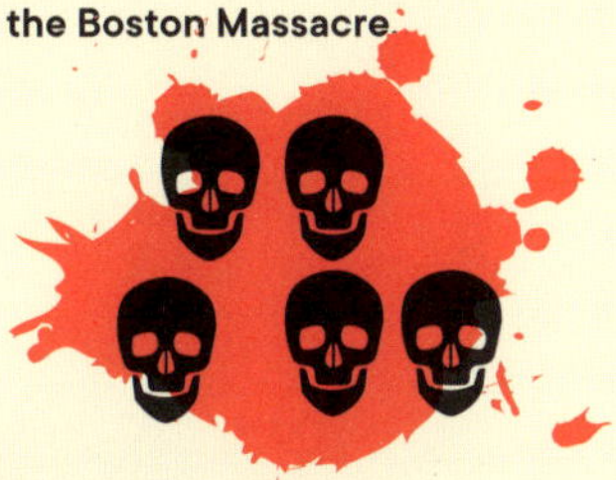

1773 During the Boston Tea Party protest British tea is dumped in the city's harbour.

1774 The first Continental Congress meets in Philadelphia.

1775

18 April Paul Revere's ride.

19 April The American War of Independence begins with the Battles of Lexington and Concord.

15 June George Washington made commander of Continental Army.

17 June Battle of Bunker Hill, the first major battle of the war.

23 August Britain's King George III declares the colonies in open rebellion.

1776

10 January Thomas Paine publishes the pamphlet *Common Sense.*

4 July Declaration of Independence adopted by 12 colonies.

1777 Congress sends Articles of Confederation to states for ratification.

1778 France and the colonies form an alliance against the British.

1781

British general Cornwallis surrenders to Washington after Siege of Yorktown.

1783 The Americans and British sign Treaty of Paris.

1787 Constitutional Convention approves the Constitution.

1788 All states (except Rhode Island & North Carolina) ratify the Constitution.

1789

4 March First US Congress under Constitution meets.

30 April Washington made first President of the United States.

1791 The 1791 Bill of Rights (first 10 amendments of Constitution) is adopted.

THE ORIGINAL AMERICANS

Native Americans are the Indigenous Peoples of Canada and the United States. They were there thousands of years before the European settlers arrived, and what is now called the USA remains their homeland.

COMING TO AMERICA

How humans may have travelled to what's now the USA...

Historians believe the ancestry of Native American tribes may go back more than 30,000 years to the first humans to live in North America.

THEORY #1

During the last ice age, around 35,700 years ago, the sea level dropped, and a land bridge called Beringia emerged. This bridge spanned the Bering Strait from Siberia to Alaska.

It's thought the bridge allowed hunters from Asia to explore territory in what's now known as North America.

Beringia disappeared underwater around 13,000 to 11,000 years later.

574

Number of Native American tribes recognised by the US government in 2025.

300

Indigenous languages spoken at time of Europeans arrival in North America.

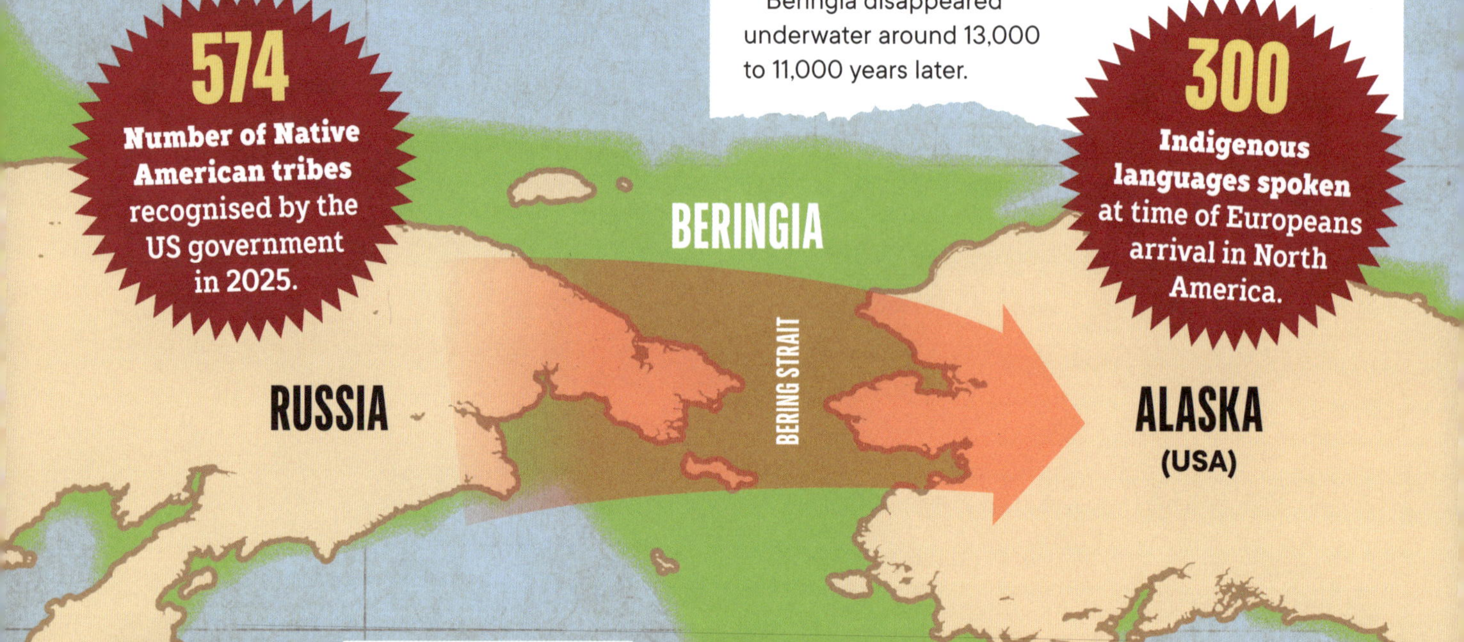

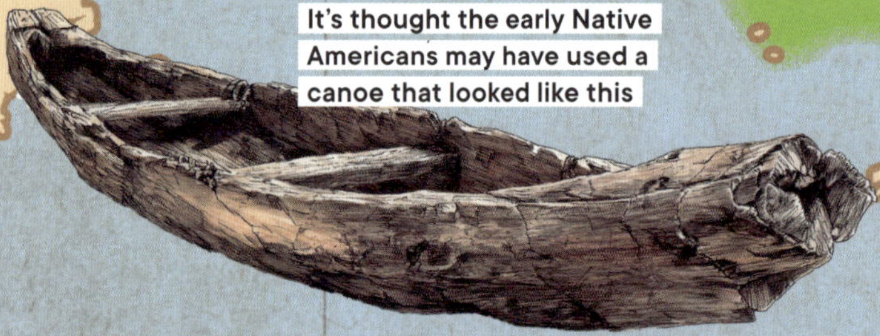

It's thought the early Native Americans may have used a canoe that looked like this

THEORY #2

Explorers may have sailed to Alaska and then travelled south along the coastline. Some evidence suggests humans were in the Americas 5,000 to 8,000 years before Beringia emerged.

EARLY LIFE

The early migrants were hunter-gatherers who lived off animals they hunted and plants they found.

Over thousands of years, as the region's climate gradually became warmer, the descendants of the first migrants settled throughout North, Central and South America.

By the 15th century, when Europeans first arrived in the Americas, it is said that there were between two million and 18 million Indigenous People in North America.

They lived in hundreds of tribes that had chiefs and priests, made art, jewellery and pots, wove baskets and cotton cloth, and built houses and canals.

Like other peoples in Asia, Europe and Africa around the same time, they grew vegetables and fruits, and crops including peanuts, cacao beans, tobacco, rubber and, importantly, maize (corn).

Artist's impression of Native Americans hunting a mastodon

Reconstruction of a Caribbean Indigenous Peoples' village

The land was owned and worked on by the whole tribe and the food was divided among everyone.

Although the people had no written language, knowledge and traditions were passed on by word of mouth.

Columbus and other European explorers found a land as populated as their own countries with well-developed cultures and traditions.

The 'Indian' question

The Italian Christopher Columbus is now celebrated as the first known European explorer to set foot on American soil.

Columbus called Native Americans, 'Indians' because he misjudged the size of the world.

He thought that his ships had landed in a part of South Asia, so he named people there 'Indios' (Spanish for those that lived in the Indus Valley).

The word 'Indian' was widely used for a Native American up until the 1960s, when activists began to reject the term as it could be considered racist.

A 16th-century engraving of Columbus landing in the Caribbean

'¡TIERRA! ¡TIERRA!'

Although he never set foot in the country we now know as the United States, Christopher Columbus is widely celebrated as the man who 'discovered' the Americas

On the morning of 12 October 1492, a Spanish sailor called Rodrigo de Triana spotted an island in the Bahamas in the Caribbean Sea and shouted '¡Tierra! ¡Tierra!' (Spanish for Land! Land!).

Rodrigo was excited because the crew had been told that the first man to spot land would be rewarded with a fortune in maravedis (Spanish coins).

However, that prize went to his boss, Italian explorer Christopher Columbus who claimed he had seen a light from the island the night before.

Columbus and the crew of his three ships were greeted by the Arawaks, the Indigenous Peoples of the Bahama Islands. The explorer named their island San Salvador ('Holy Saviour' in Spanish).

The Arawaks traded parrots, cotton and spears for the sailors' glass beads and bells, but what Columbus really wanted was gold...

Did the Vikings get there first?

According to the Norse Grænlendinga saga, around 985 CE, Viking explorer Bjarni saw land thought to be part of modern-day eastern Canada. This would make him the first European to see the Americas.

Eiríks saga rauða (Erik the Red's Saga) tells us that about 15 years later, Leif Erikson led an expedition in search of the land Bjarni had spotted.

Leif found the very icy Helluland and then went south to the warmer Vinland ('Land of Wine').

Who was Columbus?

Born Cristoforo Colombo in Genoa, Italy in 1451, the son of a weaver, Columbus was a trader and an expert sailor. The Spanish King Ferdinand II and Queen Isabella I agreed to fund Columbus's 1492 expedition to the Indies and Asia on the understanding he would bring back spices and other valuable items, the most prized of which was gold.

The royal couple gave their adventurer the title, Admiral of the Ocean Sea.

DID YOU *know?*

Columbus Day (12 October) is now a national holiday in countries throughout the Americas including the United States.

Columbus had three ships and 90 crew members.

ON SAN SALVADOR

The Spanish took some of the unarmed Arawak prisoner and demanded that they take the Conquistadors to their gold.

'We could subjugate them all and make them do whatever we want,' Columbus wrote in his log.

They sailed to the land now known as Cuba and a place they called Hispaniola (now the area known as Haiti and the Dominican Republic.)

The Spanish were excited to see traces of gold in rivers and locals presented Columbus with a mask made of gold.

The *Santa María* ran aground on Hispaniola, and its timber was used to build a fort called Navidad (Christmas), **the first European military base on what is now American soil**.

Some of the crew were left there to search for gold, while the *Niña* and the *Pinta* sailed back to Spain.

A second trip

Columbus told the Spanish king and queen that if they financed another trip he would return with gold and slaves. They gave him 17 ships and more than 1,200 men.

This new band of explorers sailed around the Caribbean taking native peoples captive along the way.

However, back on Hispaniola they found their crewmates at Fort Navidad had been killed in battles with the locals.

Artist's impression of an Arawak family

Enslaved people were sent back to Spain but many of them died on the long voyage to Europe.

Columbus sent unsuccessful expeditions into Haiti's mainland in search of **gold**.

MORE EURO SETTLERS THIS WAY

ENSLAVED!

Desperate to fulfil his promise to the Spanish royals, in the province of Cicao on Hispaniola Columbus ordered all Indigenous Peoples over the age of 14 to collect a certain amount of gold every three months.

Those that reached these targets were given copper tokens. Those without a token had their hands cut off and were left to die. Any that tried to escape their impossible task were hunted down by dogs.

It's estimated that within two years, half of the population of 250,000 had died.

Once the Spaniards had claimed the island's gold, they put locals to work as slaves on estates known as encomiendas.

Thousands of Arawaks died and the population collapsed...

BY 1515	BY 1550	BY 1650
50,000	500	☠

So began the story of Europeans' conquest of Indigenous Peoples' settlements in the Americas.

Sebastian Münster's 1540 map of the New World

THE 'NEW WORLD' ORDER

The Europeans wanted to gain control of valuable resources such as crops, animal furs and minerals in the Americas (which they called the 'New World').

The invaders did not consider Indigenous Peoples to be owners of their lands.

They looked on the Indigenous Peoples as savages who would benefit from the introduction of a European lifestyle and religion.

However, Europeans brought ruinous changes to Indigenous Peoples and their ways of life. These included accidentally introducing infectious diseases (such as smallpox, influenza, malaria, measles, typhoid and tuberculosis). Many were life-threatening to Indigenous Peoples and their populations were devastated.

Europeans enslaved large numbers of Indigenous People, seized Indigenous land and tried to destroy native cultures and religions.

INVADERS & THEIR TERRITORY

The first European countries to begin colonising the Americas were Spain and Portugal.

During the 16th century, Spain claimed Mexico, most of Central and South America, several islands in the Caribbean, and what are now Florida, California, and the south-west region of the United States. Portugal took control of Brazil.

Today, the region covered by Mexico, Central and South America, and the Caribbean islands is known as Latin America. Most of the people there speak Spanish or Portuguese.

In 1565, Spanish forces led by Pedro Menéndez de Avilés founded St Augustine in what is now Florida. This was the first successful European settlement in what was to become the United States of America. **Spain didn't colonise modern-day Texas and California until the 1700s.**

'I think I'll call it America…'

Italian explorer Amerigo Vespucci explored what Europeans called the New World between 1499 and 1502.

In 1507, German map maker Martin Waldseemüller suggested that it be called 'America' after Vespucci in tribute to the work he'd done in the territory.

At first, the name was applied to just South America but was eventually used for what we now know as North and Central America.

Amerigo Vespucci

Here to stay…

It was 1600 before other European colonists began to settle in the Americas.

In North America, **France** was the first European country to colonise Canada and the valleys of the St Lawrence, Ohio, Mississippi, and Alabama rivers.

France also took control of French Guiana in South America, and several Caribbean islands.

The Netherlands took territory in the Hudson River valley area of North America and had island territories in the Caribbean.

Sweden claimed the Delaware River valley in North America.

Russia had colonies in Alaska.

Colonisers from **England** founded 13 colonies on the Atlantic coast of North America.

Large parts of these colonies were controlled by European trading companies.

BRITISH RULE

First contact

The Italian John Cabot was the first explorer to reach North America on behalf of the British.

Cabot is thought to have landed in Newfoundland, Canada in 1497, but it would be another 100 years before English settlers tried to make the continent their home.

First colony

In 1585, the English explorer Richard Grenville landed on the coast of what would be Virginia.

The Indigenous Peoples welcomed Grenville's seven ships but when one of them stole a silver cup Grenville took this as an excuse to ransack and then burn down their village!

Jamestown in Virginia, founded in 1607, was the first English settlement. It was set up inside Native American territory.

When the colony's supplies ran low in 1610 some settlers left to join the natives. The governor asked the native chief, Powhatan, to return them. When that didn't happen, the English attacked and murdered their people.

This was the beginning of a long-running conflict, and in 1622, the Native Americans killed 347 settlers.

Not able to enslave or live alongside the Indigenous Peoples the English imposed their colony on the Native Americans by force.

4 REASONS THE BRITISH WERE THERE

1 NATURAL RESOURCES

Tobacco, sugar and other local goods for trade

2 RELIGIOUS FREEDOM

No laws on how to worship

3 POLITICAL POWER

Expansion of the British empire that rivalled that of Spain

4 NEW OPPORTUNITIES

A fresh start for rich and poor

A 1628 engraving of the 1622 massacre

Richard Grenville

Chief Powhatan

How what would become the United States of America started life as 13 colonies ruled by King George III

NEW ENGLAND

English Puritans believed it was their God-given right to take the land of the Pequots and other tribes in this region.

The English killed the Native Americans they came across and destroyed the crops in abandoned villages.

THE MAYFLOWER

The second English settlement was Plymouth, founded in 1620, in what is now the state of Massachusetts.

After a 66-day voyage across the Atlantic, the *Mayflower* – possibly the most famous ship in American history – arrived in Plymouth harbour. On board were the men, women and children of the first permanent colony in North America established by families.

Known as the **Pilgrims**, they left England because King James I did not permit freedom of religion. All James's subjects were expected to belong to the Church of England.

The Pilgrims wanted to live in a place where they could worship as they liked. They were among a group called the Puritans, protestants who favoured simple rituals and practices. Some were Separatists who believed the church should be separate from the state.

They first tried to set up a community in Leiden, Holland in 1608, but the Pilgrims struggled to make money and to retain their native language and customs. After three years of planning, they and other English Separatists set sail for Virginia on 16 September 1620.

Replica of the original Plymouth Colony

FIRST SIGNS OF REVOLUTION?

During the voyage, the men among the Pilgrims drew up and signed the MAYFLOWER COMPACT. This document stated their intention to live under 'such a government and governors as we should by common consent agree to make and choose'.

The *Mayflower* had more than 100 passengers. They survived on hard biscuits, cheese and salted beef or fish, but the lack of fresh fruit and vegetables meant many of them developed scurvy (a life-threatening disease linked to a lack of vitamin C).

It was reported that a sailor and a servant died, and that a baby was born during the stormy crossing.

The ship moored at Cape Cod, in what is now known as Provincetown Harbor on Saturday 11 November. A month later, the Pilgrims decided on the best place for their settlement and on 21 December they finally landed at Plymouth Rock, Virginia.

The Pilgrims would become a powerful force in New England.

MORE BRITS ABROAD OVERLEAF

THE 13 COLONIES

The areas under British control that turned against their home country.

The 13 British territories were established along the Atlantic coast from New England to Virginia.

Between 1625 and 1775, the settler population of the British colonies grew from just 2,000 to 2.4 million (including around 500,000 slaves).

The expansion of settler communities displaced many Native Americans.

The New England Colonies

MASSACHUSETTS

Originally founded by the Pilgrims at Plymouth in 1620, the mass settlement of British Puritans here, beginning in 1630, led to the establishment of the other New England colonies.

NEW HAMPSHIRE

First founded in 1623 at Pannaway Plantation (now Rye) by a group of 11 fishermen led by a Scot, David Thompson (Thompson Island in Boston Harbour bears his name).

RHODE ISLAND

Providence Plantations was founded by the Puritan minister Roger Williams in 1636. In 1663, a Royal Charter brought together this and three other settlements as the Rhode Island colony.

CONNECTICUT

Dutch explorers arrived in the area in 1614, and the first Brits followed in 1633. A large group of Puritans from Massachusetts established the colony of Connecticut at Hartford in 1635.

Roger Williams delivering the Royal Charter

The Southern Colonies

MARYLAND

Founded by statesman George Calvert as a haven for English Catholics in 1634.

George Calvert

NEW CAROLINA

Settled in 1653 and later made two separate colonies, **North Carolina** and **South Carolina** in 1730. They were split after it was decided that the small farms of the north and the large plantations of the south were too difficult to manage as one colony.

VIRGINIA

After Jamestown was established in 1607, the first representative legislature (or government) was set up there in 1619. The surrounding area of Virginia became a colony in 1624.

GEORGIA

Founded in 1733 by colonists led by army officer and MP James Oglethorpe, Georgia was first established at Savannah. Its main aims were to be a buffer between the Carolinas and Spanish-controlled Florida and be a place where 'unemployed and unemployable' Brits could start a new life.

FACT **VIRGINIA** WAS NAMED AFTER ENGLAND'S **QUEEN ELIZABETH I** WHO WAS KNOWN AS THE **'VIRGIN QUEEN'**.

Known for its tolerance, **RHODE ISLAND** was the first of the 13 colonies to (officially) **BAN SLAVERY**, although there is no evidence this law was enforced!

The Middle Colonies

NEW JERSEY

Claimed by the Dutch as part of New Netherlands in 1609, it was taken by the British in 1660.

NEW YORK

Also founded by the Dutch as part of New Netherlands in 1624, seized by the British in 1664.

DELAWARE

Founded by the Swedes as New Sweden in 1638, it was taken from the Dutch in 1664.

PENNSYLVANIA

Charles II gave the region to religious thinker William Penn to establish a colony of Quakers in 1681.

Mystery of the lost colony

A British colony had been established at Roanoke Island, now part of North Carolina, in 1585.

Part of an expedition sponsored by Sir Walter Raleigh, its first settlers soon abandoned their settlement, but in 1587 another group tried their luck.

By August 1590 this second colony of about 100 people had mysteriously disappeared.

The only potential clue they left behind was the word 'Crotoan' (the name of a nearby island) carved on a tree...

MORE COLONIALS THIS WAY

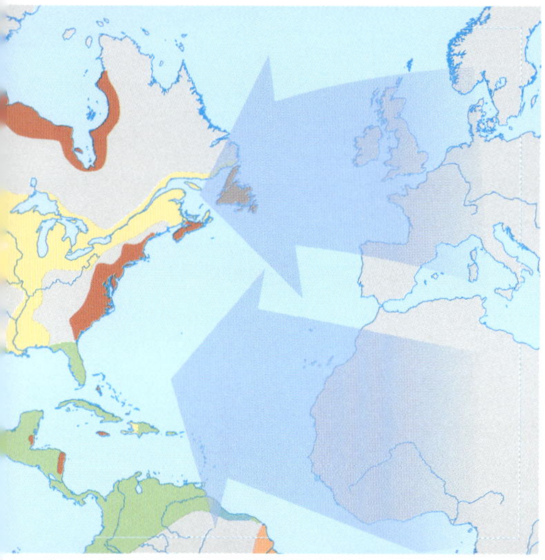

Others in the 13 colonies

The English may have ruled these colonies, but they were also home to people from many different backgrounds.

The 1600s saw the arrival of the first settlers from Germany, Bohemia, Ireland, Poland, Scotland, the Netherlands, France, Finland, Italy, Sweden and Denmark.

Of these communities, the Germans were the largest with many settling in Pennsylvania and Georgia.

Settlers' ships also brought enslaved Black people from the west coast of Africa to work in the British colonies.

The issue of slavery would be the cause of the American Civil War (1861–1865) and divide the country for hundreds of years.

The colonies had their own institutions including a colonial assembly that was their version of Britain's House of Commons. They had the power to tax and spend the money raised in the colony.

CLASH OF THE EMPIRES!

FRENCH AND INDIAN WAR
1754–1763

This war was fought between France and Britain (and their Native American allies) over the control of North American colonies.

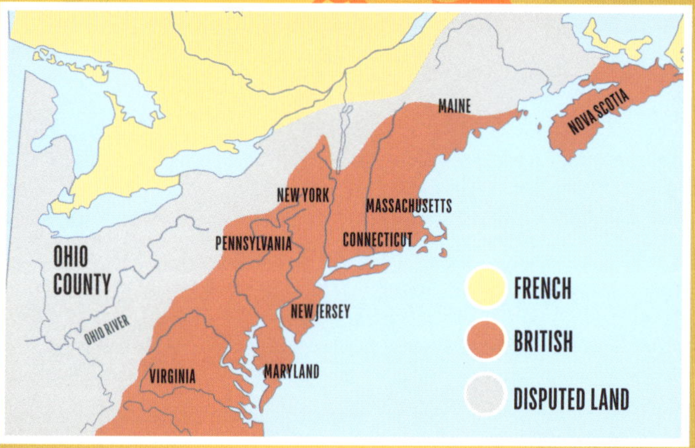

Many historians see the French and Indian War as part of the worldwide Seven Years' War.

The British and French empires came to blows over the upper Ohio River valley region. Both claimed the area as part of their territory.

Concerned by French expansion, in October 1753, Virginia's Lieutenant Governor Robert Dinwiddie sent a 21-year-old Virginia Regiment major called George Washington to deliver a message to the French demanding that they leave.

Washington's account of his journey to and from Ohio made him a celebrity in America and Britain – and that was just for starters...

A clash on the Monongahela River marked the beginning of the war. After British victories at Fort Frontenac (1758) and the Battle of the Plains of Abraham (1759), the decisive last battle was at Signal Hill in 1762.

The Treaty of Paris in 1763, gave Britain almost all of France's North American land east of the Mississippi River. It ended the threat from France but also meant the colonies were less dependent on Britain.

A young George Washington

However... the most important consequence of the war was that it **PUT BRITISH TROOPS IN THE COLONIES...**

WAR, PEACE & PROSPERITY

As the colonies grew, Britain fought two European-wide conflicts, the War of the Spanish Succession (1701–1714) and the War of the Austrian Succession (1740–1748), along with the global Seven Years' War (1756–1763).

War is expensive and a distraction for any nation, and throughout the first half of the 18th century, the cash-strapped British government neglected its colonies.

In the run up to the War of Independence, most North American colonists were loyal to the British crown, but they saw their colony as their country.

The 13 colonies were separate and unconnected. It was much easier to travel from Boston to London than it was to get from Boston to Carolina.

By the mid-1700s, the colonies were places of wealth and opportunity. Many colonists believed that their success was a result of the British government leaving them to live as they pleased.

The British Navy reported that, on average, **COLONISTS** were **TWO INCHES TALLER** than the British!

View of English Harbour on the island of Antigua

13 more to worry about...

Britain had 26 colonies in what Europeans called the New World. In terms of trade, the 13 American colonies were less important to the British than the so-called 'Sugar Islands' in the Caribbean and Atlantic.

They included **Barbados**, **Jamaica**, **Bermuda**, **Antigua**, **St Kitts** and **Grenada** and were far more profitable.

Sugar, molasses and rum were produced on these islands using slave labour.

Meanwhile back in Britain...

Members of Parliament in the more conservative Tory political party saw the colonies as a source of income via taxes that required minimal expenditure.

Those MPs in the more progressive Whig party wanted the colonies to make goods and trade with the British. They were more open to the idea of the colonies having equal status with the mother country.

The debate continued for years without a government committing to a plan for the 13 colonies. AND THAT WAS TO PROVE FATAL...

Who was the man who ruled the American colonies from 3,000 miles away?

THE LIFE & TIMES OF **KING GEORGE III**

1738 Born George William Frederick, he is said to have been a shy and emotional child.

1751 His father, Frederick Louis, dies leaving 12-year-old George heir to the British throne.

1775 George announces that the American colonists are committing treason. He feared his subjects in other British territories would rebel if the colonists won independence.

1776

In the Declaration of Independence, Thomas Jefferson calls King George a tyrant.

1781 The American colonies are lost after the British Army surrenders to George Washington at Yorktown, Virginia.

1783 George appoints 24-year-old William Pitt the Younger as Prime Minister. He helps George regain popularity in Britain.

1815 Victory over France after 12 years of the Napoleonic Wars, establishes Britain as a major world power.

1820 George dies aged 81 at Windsor Castle. His reign remains the third longest in British history.

1754 The French and Indian War begins.

1756 The Seven Years' War begins.

1760 Becomes George III, King of Great Britain. The country is at war and much of the kingdom's power is now with its quarrelling members of parliament.

1763 Britain wins the French and Indian War and is among the allies that win the Seven Years' War.

1762 The King and Queen move into Buckingham House, now Buckingham Palace.

1761 Marries Charlotte Sophia of Mecklenburg-Strelitz. Charlotte was a German protestant princess George had never met.

However, this political union turned into a happy marriage that lasted more than 50 years, and the couple had 15 children.

George III was the third Hanoverian king of Great Britain and the **first** of them **to speak English** as his **first language.**

1801 Act of Union unites Great Britain and Ireland as one country. The same year Pitt resigns after George refuses to give Catholics freedom of worship.

1807 The transatlantic slave trade is banned within the British empire.

1811 Regency period begins when his son, the future George IV, takes over on his father's behalf after George is deemed too ill to rule.

Unlike his dutiful and careful father, Prince George famously loved to party and spend money.

1810 Princess Amelia, George's youngest and favourite child, dies, aged 27.

Modern monarch

Unlike his predecessors, George was a keen patron of the arts and sciences, and his interest in agriculture earned him the nickname '**Farmer George**'.

As a devout Christian and family man, he believed it was his duty to set an example to his people.

Madness?

In 1788, King George fell seriously ill. This lasted for a year, and at one point he was restrained in a straitjacket. The king was labelled 'mad' and 'insane', and he suffered relapses in 1801 and 1810.

However, it's now believed George had a group of disorders called 'porphyria' that can cause fever, pain, confusion and hallucinations.

HOW THE BRITISH GOT

There were many causes of the American Revolution but among the biggest were the British laws and taxes imposed on the colonists...

DO AS YOU'RE TOLD!

After claiming victory in the worldwide Seven Years' War, Britain looked to its colonies to help finance its global empire.

Defending that empire was expensive and Britain's national debt was 13.5 times its annual revenue.

After he took the throne in 1760, King George III brought politicians in the Tory party into the British government.

The Tories believed the colonies should do as they were told and simply work on behalf on the empire.

Rebellious royalists?

Some in England called rebellious colonists 'royalists' because they urged the king to ignore and overrule parliament and its acts.

However, ever since the Glorious Revolution of 1688, the ruling power in Britain had been – and still is – parliament.

The monarch rules at the invitation of the people's representatives – not the other way round...

This famous slogan sums up a major cause of the American revolution.

The settlers thought it was unfair that their home country expected them to pay taxes even though they were not represented in the British parliament.

The phrase is said to date back to a pamphlet written in 1761 by Massachusetts lawyer and politician James Otis Jr.

The British argument...

was that the colonists were **'virtually represented'**, and that not all boroughs or counties in England had elected members of parliament at the time.

Also, colonists...

- paid as little as **a tenth of the tax paid by those living in Britain** at the time and
- had their **pick of cheap land** on which to build homes and establish businesses.

FACT BY **1763**, THOSE THAT LIVED IN THE 13 COLONIES WERE COMMONLY **REFERRED TO AS 'AMERICAN'**, THERE AND IN BRITAIN

IT WRONG IN 9 ACTS

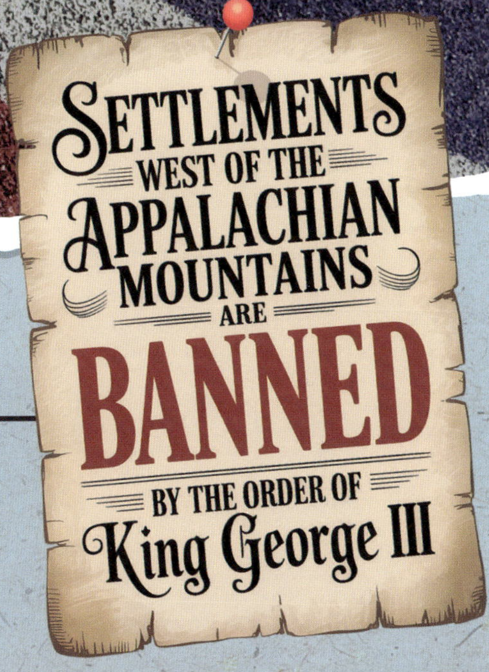

ROYAL PROCLAMATION (1763)

In an attempt to limit conflicts with Native Americans, settlements west of the Appalachian Mountains were banned.

This was done by order of George III, not parliament. Colonists were not pleased. They had successfully fought alongside the British in the French and Indian War (1754–63) so they could claim this territory.

The British saw peace with the Indigenous Peoples as crucial to a secure future for the colonies.

SUGAR ACT (1764) ACT 1

The smuggling of molasses was a major problem in the colony of New England. The taxes on this sticky sweet stuff were halved but the British came down harder on smugglers.

Those caught were tried by British government officials in vice-admiralty courts and not by juries made up of other colonists.

CURRENCY ACT (1764) ACT 2

Colonies were banned from producing paper money. This was tough on colonists because times were hard after the French and Indian War and money was scarce. The act made doing business with other countries more difficult.

STAMP ACT (1765) ACT 3

This act required many paper documents and products to be stamped to show a duty (tax) had been paid. They included newspapers, pamphlets, diplomas, legal documents and even playing cards.

This was the first direct tax on colonists imposed by the British parliament. Previously, the colonies had been taxed indirectly via custom duties.

THE STAMP ACT HAD THE MOST IMPACT

IT DIRECTLY AFFECTED PEOPLE AT ALL LEVELS THROUGHOUT THE COLONIES AND MET WIDESPREAD RESISTANCE.

Virginia Resolves

In May 1765, the House of Burgesses (the lower house of the Virginia General Assembly) passed The Virginia Resolves.

These said that colonists were entitled to 'all the liberties, privileges, franchises and immunities... possessed by the people of Great Britain' and they should be treated the same as other British people.

A printed version also stated only the Virginia assembly had the right to tax the colony and that anyone who disagreed was an enemy!

These ideas helped radicalise other colonies.

MORE

Stamp Act Congress

In October 1765, delegates from nine of the colonies met in New York.

The congress issued a **Declaration of Rights and Grievances** that declared their allegiance to George III and respect for the British parliament.

However, like the Virginia Resolves, it also stated the colonists should have the same rights as Britons.

These rights included trial by jury and the right to be taxed only by their own elected representatives.

One of the delegates, future Founding Father Benjamin Franklin said the right not to be taxed without consent was the 'prime maxim of all free government'.

THE QUARTERING ACT (1765)

ACT 4

In May of 1765, parliament passed an act that stated colonists had to provide British soldiers with a place to stay and supplies as required. Coming just two months after the Stamp Act, this only added to the discontent in the colonies.

THE PEOPLE'S PROTEST

The most important acts of resistance to the Stamp Act were those of **ordinary people.**

Rebellious Bostonians

Riots broke out in Boston, Massachusetts.

- Crowds burned an effigy (doll) of Andrew Oliver, the British government's stamp distributor for the colony, and a building he owned was pulled down. Oliver resigned the next day.
- The following week, a mob caused damage to the home of his brother-in-law, Lieutenant Governor Thomas Hutchinson, a vocal supporter of the Stamp Act (although in private he warned the British against it!).

Impossible act

By November 1765, all 12 British stamp distributors had resigned and the act became impossible to enforce.

Merchants fight back

In protest against the act, many merchants in the colonies refused to import goods from Britain.

They hoped this would lead British merchants to put pressure on their government to repeal (remove) the act.

Their plan worked. In January 1766, London-based merchants sent a letter to parliament complaining the act was ruining their businesses!

VIOLENCE AND INTIMIDATION SPREAD THROUGHOUT THE COLONIES

As we shall see, the people of Boston would go on to play a crucial part in the American Revolution...

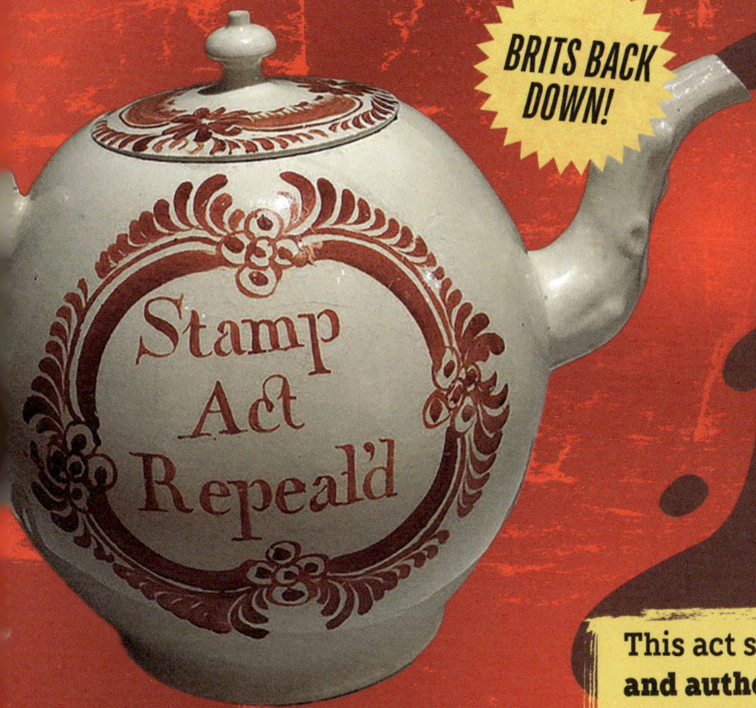

BRITS BACK DOWN!

DECLARATORY ACT (1766)

ACT 5

In February 1766, after the merchants had complained, parliament repealed the Stamp Act and the colonists celebrated.

Protesters even made their own commemorative merch – including a teapot.

And in New York City, locals raised a statue of King George III in honour of the act being repealed.

However...

To save face and to avoid this kind of problem in the future, the British parliament passed the Declaratory Act.

This act stated that parliament had the **'full power and authority to make laws . . . to bind the colonies and people of America . . . in all cases whatsoever'.**

TOWNSHEND ACTS (1767)

ACTS 6-9

Britain still needed revenue from its colonies. So, in June 1767, the four Townshend Acts imposed customs duties on many everyday items. These included lead, glass, paint and tea. To administrate these taxes, new American Board of Customs Commissioners was appointed, and more vice-admiralty courts were set up to try smugglers.

Customs officers and other officials (including governors, the big bosses of the colonies) were paid with money raised from illegal goods that were seized. This made them keen to catch tax dodgers, and these British officials became more powerful than the colonies own assemblies.

Why Townshend?

The four acts were championed by Charles Townshend, Britain's Chancellor of the Exchequer (i.e. head of finance)

They proved to be Townshend's last significant contribution in politics – he died suddenly in September 1767 of a fever.

TAXES ON...

GLASS

TEA

LEAD

PAINT

MORE

RENEWED RESISTANCE

Merchants boycotted British imports again. Colonists signed agreements not to buy any British goods. Their names were published in newspapers and this put pressure on those who had not signed.

Spinning clubs were formed and colonists took to wearing simple, homespun clothing.

Those that did not join the boycott were **named and shamed** in newspapers.

A network of Committees of Correspondence kept colonists in different areas up to date on different forms of protest.

These acts of resistance helped bring the colonists together in a common cause against the British.

LETTERS FROM A FARMER IN PENNSYLVANIA

In December 1767, the first of 12 essays addressed to 'the Inhabitants of the British Colonies' were published...

These 'letters' were written in the voice of a fictional farmer. A modest and well-informed man, the farmer expressed support for Britain's right to oversee trade to and from the colonies but opposed its taxes on the colonists.

A typical passage from the letters read...

'If the parliament succeeds in this attempt, other statutes will impose other duties [...] and thus the parliament will levy upon us such sums of money as they choose to take, without any other LIMITATION than their PLEASURE'

The mild-mannered farmer did not want the colonists to break away from Britain or resort to violence. As he wrote...

'Let us behave like dutiful children who have received unmerited blows from a beloved parent.'

Signed A. Farmer the 'letters' were the work of the lawyer John Dickinson.

Why were these letters important?

1. The letters appeared in many colonial newspapers and were **WIDELY READ.**
2. They were among the **MAIN REASONS** opinion turned against the Townshend Acts.
3. **TAVERNS HAD COPIES** for customers to read, and the letters would have been among the printed articles **READ OUT** to groups of people.
4. These readings meant everyone, including **THE ILLITERATE, HAD ACCESS TO INFORMATION** and to contribute to debates.
5. The letters **MADE DICKINSON FAMOUS** in the colonies, and he became known as the **'PENMAN OF THE REVOLUTION'.**
6. They also inspired fellow pamphleteer, the British-born **THOMAS PAINE** – much more on him later...

WHO WAS JOHN DICKINSON?

WAS HE A FARMER?

No.

WHO WAS HE, THEN?

- John was born to a wealthy family in Maryland in 1732.
- Eight years later, the Dickinsons moved to Dover in Delaware where they owned a plantation and put slaves to work.
- John studied law in London and was a lawyer in Philadelphia, from 1757 to 1760.
- One of the colonies' wealthiest men, Dickinson represented Pennsylvania at 1765's Stamp Act Congress and was the main author of its 'Declaration of Rights and Grievances'.
- He was accused of being a loyalist after he voted against and refused to sign the Declaration of Independence of 1776. At that point, Dickinson hoped agreement could be reached with the British.
- He later fought with the Pennsylvania militia against the British.
- Also in 1776, Dickinson freed the slaves on his family's Delaware plantation.
- He served as a representative after the war and was among those who signed the US Constitution.
- Thomas Jefferson, Founding Father and third president of the United States called Dickinson...

'ONE OF THE GREAT WORTHIES OF THE REVOLUTION.'

However...

Britain remained determined to reform and tax its American colonies...

THE BOSTON MASSACRE

The Massachusetts port was a hotbed of colonial unrest and that resistance sparked a revolution...

WHY SO ANGRY, BOSTON?

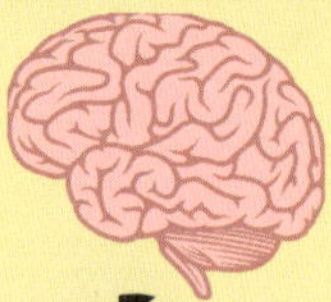

- The colonists of Massachusetts were **committed to self-governance**.
- Its leaders were **clever** and **articulate**.
- Boston was a port that was **dependent on trade** from Europe.
- **Smuggling** and the avoidance of tax was common.
- The local **press was very active** and widely read.
- In Boston, there was a **tradition of protest** on the street and in town meetings.
- The **British thinking** was if they subdued opposition in Boston that would stop the spread of rebellion across the other colonies.

The *Liberty* Affair

The *Liberty* was a ship owned by wealthy merchant and future Founding Father John Hancock.

In June 1768, it was alleged that a customs official was locked in the *Liberty*'s hold while locals – ignoring the Townshend Acts – unloaded its cargo of Madeira wine at the port of Boston.

Hancock was charged with smuggling and the *Liberty* was confiscated. The charges were later dropped but the ship was not returned.

Angry locals attacked two custom officials involved in the case, vandalised their homes and burnt a boat that belonged to one of them.

The officials fled to a British warship docked in Boston's Harbour.

Reinforcements

In October 1768, Britain sent its 14th and 29th regiments to Boston to help enforce the Townshend Acts, protect British officials from harassment and stop vandalism.

This added to feelings of unrest among Bostonians. By early 1770, protesters, including the Sons of Liberty, had turned their anger on business owners who were ignoring the boycott of British goods.

THE DEATH OF CHRISTOPHER SEIDER

On 22 February 1770 Ebenezer Richardson tried to take down a sign on a shop that identified its owner, Theophilus Lillie, as an 'importer'.

Richardson – who was known to work for the British as an informer – was attacked by a gang of boys. After he fled back to his nearby home, Richardson's front door and windows were broken.

Richardson and his friend George Wilmont then took up muskets and confronted the boys in the backyard. A shot fired by Richardson hit 11-year-old Christopher Seider (sometimes reported as Snyder or Snider), and the boy died from his wounds later that day.

It's said that the only thing that stopped angry locals from launching a revenge attack was the belief that Richardson would be convicted of his crime.

At his trial, the judges wanted Richardson to be convicted of manslaughter. But the jury found him guilty of murder, a crime that carried the death penalty.

Yet the judges refused to sentence Richardson, and, after the King granted him a royal pardon, he was released.

The case caused widespread anger among colonists.

Workers v soldiers

In early March, soon after 2,000 people had attended Seider's funeral, rope makers fought with soldiers in Boston's South End.

The British believed one of their sergeants had been murdered during the clashes, and troops were sent to search for his body at a rope works owned by John Gray.

Fearing his workers would be attacked, Gray came to an agreement with British officer Colonel William Dalrymple that both sides should stand down.

WHAT HAPPENED NEXT...

THE MASSACRE

TENSIONS WERE HIGH AND RUMOURS SWIRLED...

Among them was the belief that the British Army planned to cut down the town's Liberty Tree, a prominent symbol of the colonists' struggle.

On 5 March, a crowd attacked the barracks of the Army's 29th Regiment. Alarm bells rang out but the British did not react.

At the same time, a crowd of 50 to 60 people began throwing snowballs at the young sentry on duty outside the town's Custom House.

In response, seven soldiers marched through the mob to help the sentry. The crowd knew that before firing their guns, the soldiers were required by law to read The Riot Act. The protesters would then have an hour to disperse before weapons could be used.

The mob grew increasingly hostile, taunting the soldiers, pelting them with snow, ice and oyster shells, and daring them to shoot.

One of the soldiers, fearing for his life, fired his musket. Other soldiers, thinking the command to fire had been given, also opened fire.

Three members of the crowd were shot and killed. Eight others were wounded, and two of them died later.

- Lieutenant Governor Thomas Hutchinson ordered the soldiers back to their barracks and promised the crowd that justice would be done.
- The sentry, the seven other soldiers and their commanding officer, Captain Thomas Preston, were arrested.
- After a town meeting demanded the removal of troops, the two British regiments were moved to Castle William (now Castle Island) in Boston's harbour.

FIRST CASUALTY OF THE REVOLUTION

Crispus Attucks was the first victim of the Boston Massacre and the first casualty of the American Revolution.

Aged 27 and a sailor at the time of his death, little is known about Crispus's life.

It's thought that his father was Black and his mother Native American, and that Crispus had escaped slavery before he went to sea.

For many, Crispus Attucks is a national hero. There is a monument to him on Boston Common and public buildings have been named in his honour.

Nearly two centuries later, US civil rights leader Rev Dr Martin Luther King Jr wrote, *'He is one of the most important figures in African-American history, not for what he did for his own race but for what he did for all oppressed people everywhere.'*

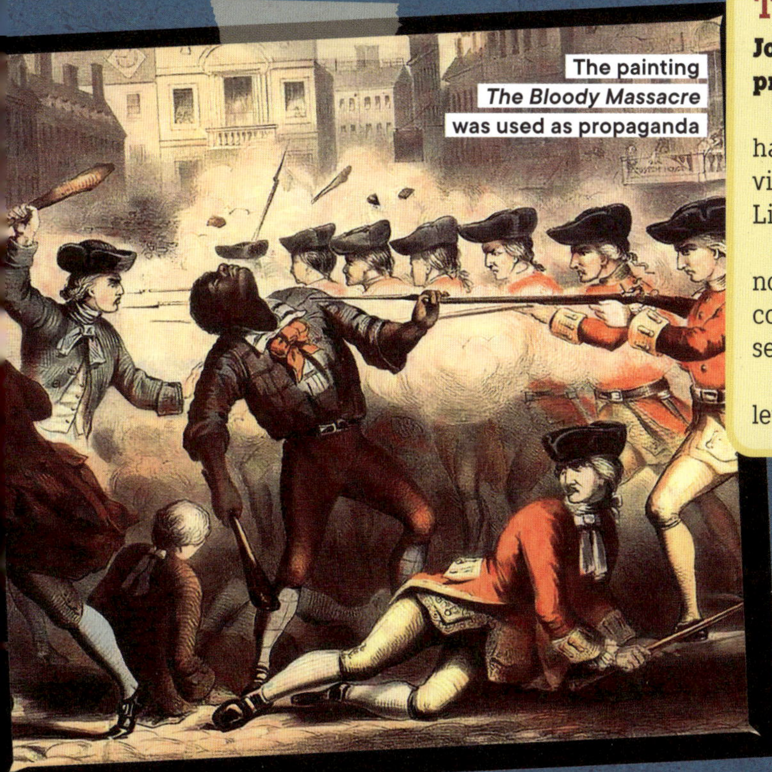

The painting *The Bloody Massacre* was used as propaganda

AFTERMATH

- **Both sides were quick to publicise their version of what happened on the night of 5 March.**
- There were reports, poems, newspaper articles and a famous painting by Henry Pelham: *The Fruits of Arbitrary Power* also known as *The Bloody Massacre*.
- This was reproduced as an engraving and widely distributed – without crediting Pelham! – by a Boston silversmith named Paul Revere (more on him later...).
- It wasn't entirely accurate – it showed a row of soldiers firing at the same time into the crowd – but as a piece of propaganda it was extremely effective and increased support for the colonists' cause.

Branding was a form of punishment

Trials

John Adams, a future Founding Father and US president, was one of the soldiers' defence lawyers.

Adams was keen to uphold the principle of everyone having the right to a fair trial. He also opposed the violent tactics of protesters such as the Sons of Liberty, led by his cousin Samuel Adams.

After John Adams established that there was no evidence of a command to fire being given, commanding officer Preston was acquitted and, at a separate trial, just two of the soldiers were convicted.

Their punishment was the branding of a permanent letter 'M' (for 'manslaughter') at the base of a thumb.

Brits back down again!

In April 1770, the British parliament repealed all the new duties except the one on tea. This was to save face and retain the right to tax colonists. This may have been seen as a safe option but, as we'll see, it was anything but...

THE TEA ACT

The British parliament's Tea Act of May 1773 granted the East India Company a monopoly on tea exports to the colonies.

The company had millions of pounds worth of unsold tea sitting in warehouses and was in big financial trouble.

The act meant it could supply Americans with tea at a low price that would undercut the smuggled version they were used to.

This British tea was cheaper, but in buying it colonists would be paying duty and, in effect, accepting parliament's right to tax them.

Not surprisingly, this infuriated merchants and supporters of independence.

THE BOSTON TEA PARTY

It may be the most famous protest in the history of the United States but it was no 'party' for those involved

Before the 'party'

- After the repeal of almost all the Townshend Acts in 1770, there was a **period of calm** in the colonies, and their economy started to improve.
- Enterprising American merchants got around the duty on British tea by **buying supplies from smugglers.**
- Known as **'Dutch tea'** it's likely to have come from **several different European countries.**
- However, this uneasy **peace would not last for long...**

How the protest began...

The Tea Act stated that the duty had to be paid when a ship was unloaded.

In many places orders were cancelled and colonists refused to handle consignments.

However, in Boston, Lieutenant Governor Thomas Hutchinson (remember him?) insisted that tea from three British ships – the *Dartmouth*, *Eleanor* and *Beaver* – moored there should be unloaded...

EAST INDIA COMPANY

Founded in 1600.

Given exclusive trade rights in the East by **Elizabeth I**.

Fought wars with its **own army and imposed taxes**. At its peak, it was so huge and powerful it **operated as if it were a separate nation**.

Dissolved in 1874.

£18,000

The **1773** value of the tea destroyed

£3.5 million

Its equivalent value **today**

THE PARTY...

On the night of 16 December 1773, a mob of protesters encouraged a group of around 60 men dressed as Native Americans to board the ships and dump their cargo of 342 chests of tea into Boston's Harbour.

THE *Boston* GAZETTE

'A NUMBER OF **BRAVE & RESOLUTE MEN**, DETERMINED TO DO ALL IN THEIR POWER TO **SAVE THEIR COUNTRY FROM THE RUIN** WHICH THEIR ENEMIES HAD PLOTTED, IN LESS THAN FOUR HOURS, **EMPTIED EVERY CHEST OF TEA** ON BOARD THE THREE SHIPS..'

MORE

What's with the fancy dress?

It has been said that the protesters dressed as Native Americans to protect their identities, and some have suggested that they were trying to lay responsibility for the tea's destruction on Indigenous Peoples.

This is very unlikely. The costumes were very basic and thought to be symbolic. They sent a message to the British that the protesters were American, not subjects of George III and closer to Indigenous Peoples than Britons.

Bad move?

Not all colonists were impressed by the Boston protest.

Future Founding Fathers Benjamin Franklin and George Washington were among those who thought this destruction of private property could damage their cause as it allowed the British to condemn the colonists as a criminal mob.

Copycat dumps

News of the Boston protest spread throughout the colonies and inspired patriots in Charleston, Philadelphia, New York and several other smaller places to dump or confiscate tea throughout the following year.

Re-brand!

At the time, the protest was known as the 'Destruction of the Tea'.

The protest was only given its more 'fun' name of the Boston Tea Party during the mid 1820s.

By then those who had taken part were starting to die off and their protest was celebrated as an important episode in US history.

THE BRITS REACT

For many British politicians this attack on valuable property at such a huge scale was an outrage and a challenge to their power that had to be punished.

The Prime Minister Lord North said, 'We are now to establish our authority or give it up forever'.

Between March and June of 1774, the British parliament passed what its members called the **Coercive Acts** and colonists dubbed the **Intolerable** or **Insufferable Acts**.

The main aim of these acts was to punish the town of Boston and the colony of Massachusetts.

THE COERCIVE ACTS

1 BOSTON PORT ACT

Shut down the harbour and stopped all trade to and from the town.

2 MASSACHUSETTS GOVERNMENT ACT

Put the colony under the control of the British government and restricted town meetings.

3 ADMINISTRATION OF JUSTICE ACT

Stated any British official accused of a crime should be tried in Britain not Massachusetts.

George Washington called it the 'Murder Act' because he saw it as granting British officials permission to break laws knowing they were unlikely to be punished.

4 QUARTERING ACT

Forced colonists to provide housing for British soldiers.

5 QUEBEC ACT

Reset boundaries of Canada's Province of Quebec to take in the Ohio Country and other contested mid-western territories.

And a new ruler too...

General Thomas Gage, Commander in Chief of the British Army in North America, was made Governor of Massachusetts.

'THEY CAN HURT NOBODY BUT THEMSELVES'

British Prime Minister Lord North on colonists' reaction to the Coercive Acts. How wrong he was...

'WE ASK FOR PEACE,

Britain aimed to put colonists in their place with the Coercive Acts. However, what they did was to bring colonists together

JOHN ADAMS

'A VIRTUAL DECLARATION OF WAR'

In Massachusetts, colonists said The Coercive Acts were a 'virtual declaration of war'.

- They and many of their fellow British Americans now saw armed conflict with their home country as inevitable.
- Supporters throughout the 13 colonies sent supplies to Boston.
- The House of Burgesses in Virginia – the wealthiest and most powerful colony – called for a day of prayer and fasting to show its support.
- In Massachusetts, a Provincial Congress was created, and, within a year, it took control of the colony's local authorities and courts.
- By the middle of 1774, all colonies (except Georgia) had some form of local government that did the job previously done by British officials on behalf of George III.

Each colony had its own issues and demands but they were united against Britain's aggressive government.

THE FIRST CONTINENTAL CONGRESS

In response to the Coercive Acts, almost all the colonies agreed to send representatives to a national assembly. So, in September 1774, 55 delegates from 12 of the 13 colonies met in Philadelphia.

Delegates at prayer during the congress

TOP SECRET!

1. **GEORGIA DIDN'T SEND DELEGATES** because it was thought they may soon be at war with local indigenous tribes and for that they would need the backing of the British.
2. **DELEGATES WERE ELECTED** in local elections, via the colony's local assembly (if they had one) or their Committee of Correspondence.
3. **THREE FUTURE FOUNDING FATHERS** attended. They were leaders who had been important to the colonists' cause so far and would be central to the creation of the United States – **Samuel Adams, John Adams and George Washington**.

In secret, the delegates debated the future of the colonies for six weeks (5 September to 26 October 1774).

LIBERTY & SAFETY'

THE SUFFOLK RESOLVES

On 9 September 1774, a series of resolutions were agreed by leaders in Suffolk County, Massachusetts, the county that includes Boston. They recommended...

- ✗ **BOYCOTTING** BRITISH IMPORTS
- ✗ **REFUSING** TO PAY BRITISH TAXES
- ✓ **STOCKPILING** WEAPONS
- ✓ **REGULAR TRAINING** FOR THE LOCAL MILITIA
- ✗ **IGNORING** THE MASSACHUSETTS GOVERNMENT ACT

Future American folk hero Paul Revere took the resolves to the First Continental Congress where they were endorsed by other colonies' leaders.

THIS WAS THE MOMENT COLONISTS REALLY STARTED TO PREPARE FOR WAR....

Declaration of Rights

Out of their discussions came this document that summarised the patriots' arguments and demands. Above all, they wanted the right to be taxed by their own elected politicians (not the British) and the right to a trial by jury.

Continental Association

This document recommended that there should be a Committee of Inspection in each colony. Made up of everyday colonists, they would police their own communities.

- Delegates also agreed to boycott trade with Britain (apart from exports of rice) and 'wholly discontinue the slave trade.'
- The Congress agreed Britain should continue to regulate business in its American colonies.

WHAT HAPPENED NEXT?

- The British had closed the courts, so laws were difficult to uphold.
- British rule of the colonies had ended in all but name.
- Feeling empowered by the Continental Congress, gangs of patriots marched through villages and towns in search of those still loyal to the British crown.
- Under threat of being tarred and feathered, their enemies were forced to swear allegiance to the people of the colonies.

By November 1774, King George III was in no doubt that war with his American colonies was inevitable. He told his Prime Minister Lord North that...

the rude bridge that arche
Their flag to April's breeze un
Here once the embattled farmer
And fired the shot heard round

CHAPTER 2

IT'S WAR!

How the colonists slid into war with their British rulers and emerged triumphant!

'THE BRITISH ARE COMING!'

The myths and the truth about the most famous horse ride in American history

A system of signals

In their Suffolk Resolves, the rebels of Massachusetts had openly declared their intention to stockpile arms.

Because the patriots of Boston expected the British to take action and try to seize or destroy their supplies, a **system of signals was agreed.**

- When British troops were on the move, lanterns would be put in the windows of the tower of North Church in Boston.
- **One lantern** meant that the British were on the march.
- **Two lanterns** meant they were travelling by sea.

A messenger on horseback would then alert the local militias.

THE MYTH

Paul Revere was the principal messenger for the Boston Committee of Safety, which monitored the movements of the British army.

In 1860, Henry Wadsworth Longfellow wrote the poem *Paul Revere's Ride* about events on the night of 18 April 1775.

Longfellow's is the best-known version of the story and made Revere an American folk hero, but it's not entirely accurate...

It's said Longfellow deliberately strayed from the truth because he wanted to make Revere into a legendary and heroic figure in American history.

✗ **In the poem, Revere sees a signal and rides off to warn the militia in the local areas where muskets, cannons and gunpowder had been stored.**

✗ **At 1am, Revere gets to Lexington, and at 2am he arrives in Concord. Job done.**

I DIDN'T SAY THAT!

It's a common myth that Revere yelled **'the British are coming!'** to alert his fellow patriots. In his own account, Revere said he told townsfolk, **'The Regulars [British troops] are coming out!'.**

BEAUTY MYTH

The poem mentions Revere's horse, Brown Beauty. However, there is no historical evidence that Revere owned a horse of this name, and he may well have borrowed a horse for his 'midnight ride'.

Who was Paul Revere?

Born in Boston in around 1735, Paul was the son of Apollos Rivoire, a French Huguenot (protestant) whose family had settled in Massachusetts when he was a child.

Apollos became a silversmith, and he passed on his trade to Paul.

- A gifted artisan, among other things Paul was a skilled engraver (see the Boston Massacre for more on that).
- He was a prime mover among Massachusetts patriots and seen as the link between tradespeople and the movement's more intellectual leaders.
- Revere was among the protesters who dumped British ships' cargo at the Boston Tea Party.
- During the war, Revere ran a gunpowder mill and served as a Lieutenant Colonel in the Continental Army.
- Once independence had been won, he set up a firm to manufacture copper sheets. Revere Copper is still trading today as an employee-owned company.

THE TRUTH

- ✔ **In Revere's own account of that night, he says he was one of three riders.**
- ✔ **This was because their mission was too important to be left to just one rider.**
- ✔ **Revere and William Dawes rode out from Boston. After warning the rebels at Lexington they were joined by a third rider, Dr Samuel Prescott.**
- ✔ **Revere says after leaving Lexington he was captured by the British and it was Prescott who warned the rebels of Concord.**

'THE SHOT HEARD ROUND THE WORLD'

The Continental Congress was due to meet again in May 1775, but before then events took over, and the British and the colonists went to war...

PREPARING FOR WAR...

As good as their word, the militias made up of ordinary people of Massachusetts had started to stockpile weapons and ammunition.

In response, on 19 April 1775, the British sent approximately 900 soldiers to raid militia storehouses in Concord – 18 miles outside of Boston – and stop armed conflict before it began...

Battle of Lexington

Six miles away from Concord, at Lexington Green, the British troops were met by around 50 armed militia – known as minutemen. **It was here that the first skirmish of the American Revolutionary War took place and 'the shot heard round the world' was fired.**

WHERE 'THE SHOT' CAME FROM

Now familiar to millions, this famous phrase wasn't mentioned in connection with the War of Independence for another 62 years.

In 1837 Ralph Waldo Emerson, a popular writer who lived in Concord, wrote the *Concord Hymn* for a Fourth of July celebration.

The poem is a romanticised version of the battles at Lexington and Concord. Its famous first four lines are...

By the rude bridge that arched the flood,
Their flag to April's breeze unfurled,
Here once the embattled farmers stood,
And fired the shot heard round the world

The same phrase has since been used in reference to the 1914 assassination of Archduke Franz Ferdinand that started World War I, a home run hit by the New York Giants' Bobby Thomson in a 1934 baseball game and many other (mainly sporting) moments.

Battle of Concord

Not surprisingly, the British Army overwhelmed the Lexington rebels.

However...

News of the battle at Lexington spread and other local minutemen quickly joined the ranks and readied themselves for a fight.

When a company of around 100 British soldiers marched on to Concord they were met at the town's bridge by approximately 500 militiamen.

The rebels forced the British back to Boston.

The British lost 73 men and 50 rebels died at Lexington and Concord.

Within weeks around 20,000 militia members had surrounded Boston, trapping the British regiments....

MILITIA

An army made up of civilians. All men of the colonies were trained to use a musket to protect their communities

WHY MINUTEMEN?

Because they promised to be ready for military action at a minute's warning!

EACH SIDE HAD THEIR OWN VERSION OF EVENTS

BRITISH	COLONISTS
Claimed colonists fired first and cut off scalps of dead soldiers!	Claimed the Brits fired first, without provocation, and killed unarmed locals in their own homes!

The colonists hoped George III would intervene. They sent their account to him on a ship that arrived in England two weeks before the British Army's report.

AMERICA'S FIRST ARMY

By 1775, armed conflict was inevitable and to fight a war the colonists needed an official military force

THE SECOND CONTINENTAL CONGRESS

At their meeting in May 1775, delegates were asked by leaders from Massachusetts (including John Adams, Samuel Adams and John Hancock) to support their militia.

At the time, Boston was occupied by more than 5,000 British troops, surrounded by militia from Massachusetts, Rhode Island, New Hampshire and Connecticut.

Those from the Middle Colonies such as New York, New Jersey and Philadelphia pushed for negotiating with the British.

However, the rebels won the argument and the Congress agreed to form a Continental Army that included the Massachusetts militia.

One last push for peace

In its Declaration of the **Causes of Necessity of Taking Up Arms**, the Congress explained why it was prepared to go to war.

Moderate delegates put together an **Olive Branch Petition** to be sent to the King. Written by John Dickinson it stated that the colonists...

> 'most ardently desire the former Harmony between (the mother country) and these Colonies.'

The petition arrived in England on 13 August 1775. However, before it arrived the King issued his own **Proclamation for Suppressing Rebellion and Sedition** in which he said colonists were being *'misled by dangerous and ill-designing men'*.

In October, having ignored the colonists' petition George III said the colonies were in *'open and avowed rebellion'*.

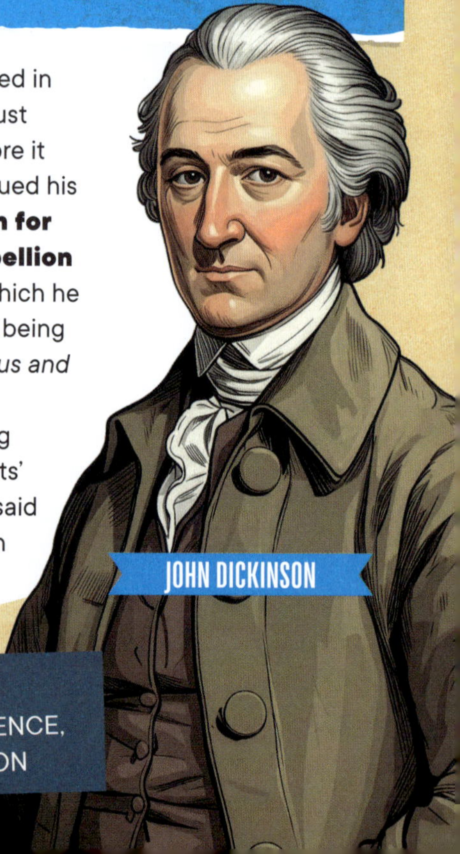

FACT

THE SECOND CONTINENTAL CONGRESS WAS, IN EFFECT, THE COLONIES' GOVERNMENT THROUGHOUT THE WAR OF INDEPENDENCE, UNTIL 1781 WHEN IT BECAME THE CONGRESS OF THE CONFEDERATION

BATTLE OF BUNKER HILL

In June 1775, Boston's minutemen set up fortifications on Breed's Hill in Charlestown, overlooking the port town.

FIRST MAJOR BATTLE!

It's said this was a mistake, and the original plan was to set up a position on the higher Bunker Hill, nearby, which gave its name to the battle to follow.

An attack on them by British Redcoats turned into the first major battle of the American Revolutionary War.

After a series of assaults, the British took the rebels' position but it cost them around 1,000 soldiers. About 450 colonists were killed.

The untrained minutemen hid behind trees, picked off the advancing troops and then retreated.

The British complained that this was an 'unfair' way to fight a battle.

Because Britain's losses were so great, Bunker Hill is often referred to as a Pyrrhic victory.

What's a Pyrrhic victory?

A victory that costs the winner so much that it could be described as a defeat.

The phrase comes from Pyrrhus of Epirus who after defeating the Romans at the Battle of Ascullum in 279 BCE is said to have exclaimed *'One more victory over the Romans and we are completely done for!'*

WHY WASHINGTON?

Two weeks after the Battle of Bunker Hill, the Continental Congress made Virginia delegate George Washington Commander in Chief of its army.

Washington was the man for the job for several reasons...

1 EXPERIENCE

Washington had commanded a Virginia Regiment during the French and Indian War.

2 CHARACTER

There were many impressive figures among the colonies' leaders but none as calm, trustworthy and dependable as Washington.

3 VIRGINIA

As a delegate from the most prosperous, and therefore most powerful colony, Washington had the support of the influential southern colonies' leaders.

4 UNITY

He added his support to the cause alongside that of other more rebellious regions in a united front against the British.

National leader

Up until this point, the 13 colonies did not have anyone who was widely regarded as their leader. Washington was the one man who it was thought could bring this new nation together.

WASHINGTON – MAN & BOY

It's often said that without George Washington, the United States would not exist, but who was the Virginian who became 'Father of the Nation'?

Early years

George was born on Popes Creek plantation in Westmoreland County, Virginia on 22 February 1732.

He was the eldest of Augustine and Mary Ball Washington's six children. Augustine also had two sons from a previous marriage.

His father was a tobacco planter and had properties throughout the colony, but the family's wealth is said to have been modest.

In 1735, Augustine moved the family to Mount Vernon, an estate later made famous by its connection with George.

His father died when George was 11, after which his older stepbrother Lawrence became a mentor to him.

George received a basic education but, unlike his two stepbrothers, he did not go to college.

It's thought this was due to the father not leaving the family much money.

THE CHERRY TREE MYTH

Another example from American history of a myth that has proved more powerful than the truth...

HOWEVER This famous story never happened. It was invented by the writer Mason Locke Weems. The myth was included in the fifth edition of Weems' bestseller, *The Life of Washington*, published in 1806.

The myth found its way into school textbooks and was taught to millions of American children as a moral tale that depicted young George as a role model to young citizens of the country he helped found.

Military leader

Like his brother Lawrence, George joined the military and by the age of 21 was a major in the Virginian militia.

As mentioned previously, the young major asked the French to leave Ohio without success, but far worse was to come... As a lieutenant colonel, he fought on behalf of the British in the French and Indian War. In 1754 Washington led an attack on a French camp. The skirmish lasted 15 minutes and left 11 dead – 10 Frenchmen and one Virginian.

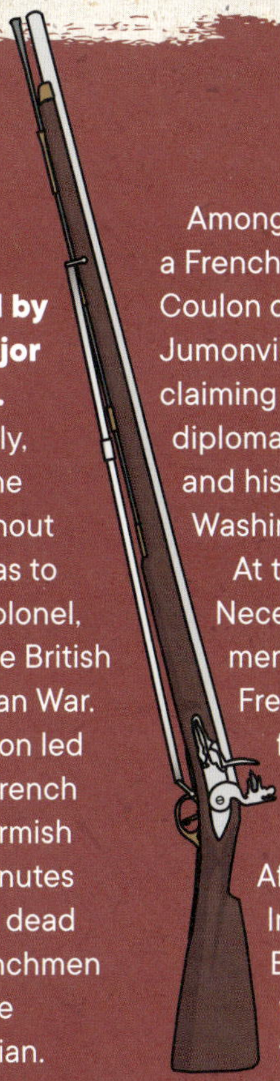

Among the fatalities was a French nobleman, Joseph Coulon de Villiers, Sieur de Jumonville. France was outraged, claiming Jumonville was a diplomat and not a soldier, and his death made Washington an assassin.

At their base, Fort Necessity, Washington's men were overwhelmed by French forces. George was forced to surrender and, by mistake, admitted to the assassination! After this, the French and Indian War spread across Europe, escalating into what became known as the Seven Years' War.

FALSE TEETH

George broke his teeth cracking walnuts, so he had to wear dentures.

It's said these false teeth were made from ivory, lead, cows' teeth and teeth pulled from the mouths of his enslaved workers!

Farmer, landowner & politician

After leaving the militia, Washington went back to work on his Virginian farm, but in 1758 he was elected as a representative in the colony's General Assembly.

The next year, George married Martha Dandridge Custis, a wealthy widow who had two young children. The couple did not have children of their own.

As a landowner, Washington was an avid reader of books on the latest farming techniques and an enthusiastic champion of agricultural innovation.

In 1766, he switched his Mount Vernon estate's main crop from tobacco to the more profitable wheat.

Slavery

Like many of the Founding Fathers, Washington supported the abolition of slavery in theory, but did little to make it happen.

George inherited 10 enslaved people from his father, and during his lifetime he would control a total of 557 enslaved people. His will stated that the slaves attached to the family should be freed after his wife's death. As it was, Martha freed them a year before her death in 1802.

WHAT THEY WORE when they went to war

THE BRITISH ARMY

Why 'Redcoats'?

First off, it's not true that the British soldiers wore a red coat because it didn't show blood (it did).

One explanation is that during the 17th century the red material used was cheaper than other options.

By the 18th century, the colour was associated with the British, had become a tradition and gave the soldiers their nickname.

Men in uniform

With an average age of 27, most British soldiers were trained and experienced in warfare.

They and their officers took great pride in the uniform. It told the enemy, civilians and potential recruits that here was a professional and formidable force.

Regiments had their own tailors and cobblers who made standard-sized uniforms and shoes to fit individual soldiers.

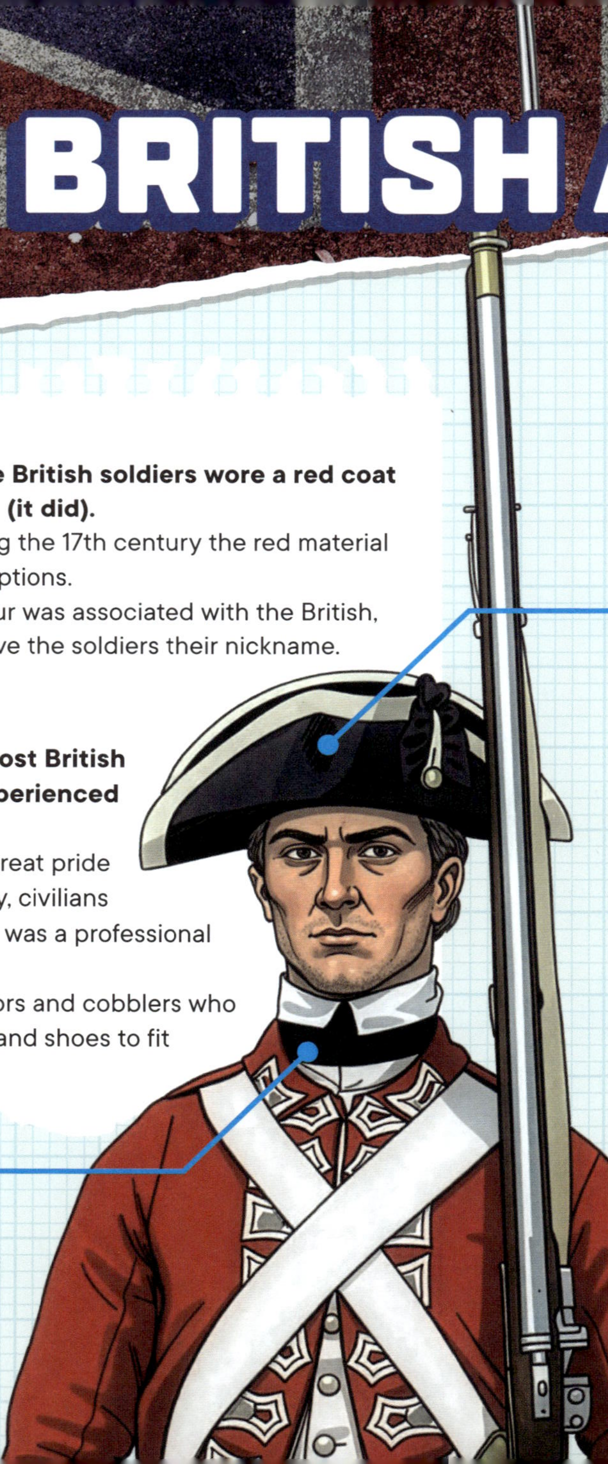

NECK STOCK

This was a black cloth, made of horsehair or velvet, worn around the neck to cover the shirt's raised collar and fastened with a brass buckle or clasp.

HAIR

- Those with impressive long locks wore them tied at the back in a club.
- Unfortunates who were bald or too malnourished to grow good strong hair were issued with a wig.
- Grease and powder (sometimes flour) were applied to combat lice.

HAT

- Styles changed throughout the 18th century but during the 1770s troops wore a hat that was **cocked** (pinned up) at the front, back and on the wearer's left.
- Made of stiff **wool-felt**, it had white worsted at the edges and a black cockade (knot) of horsehair that was worn over the left ear.
- Some added **tassels, pompoms, a regimental button or ostrich feathers.**

COAT

- It was made from 'broadcloth', a heavy fabric made from wool.
- Lapels and sleeve cuffs were made in the colour of the soldier's regiment.
- Officers' uniforms would be made of better quality materials, often by their own personal tailor.
- Troops were issued with a new coat every year. The old ones were recycled into red forage hats.

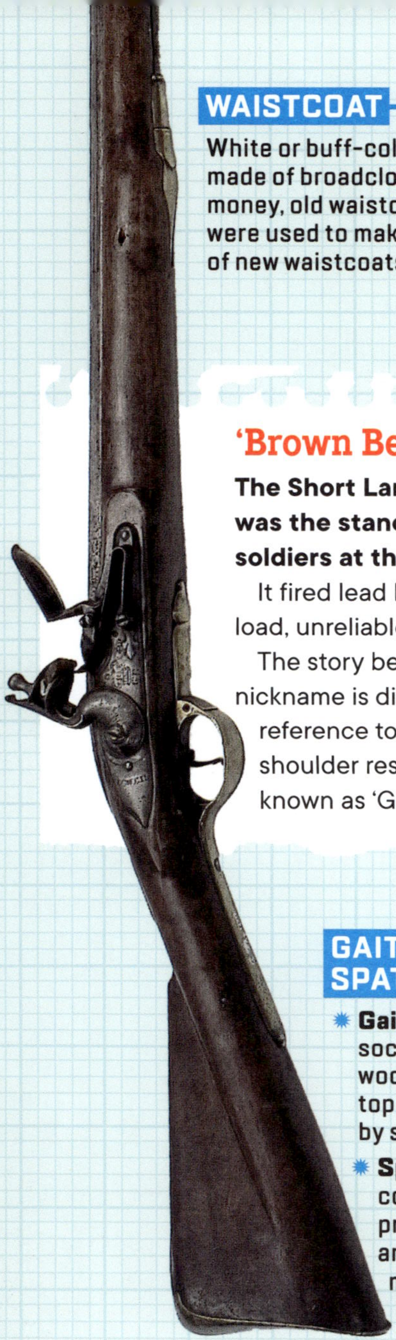

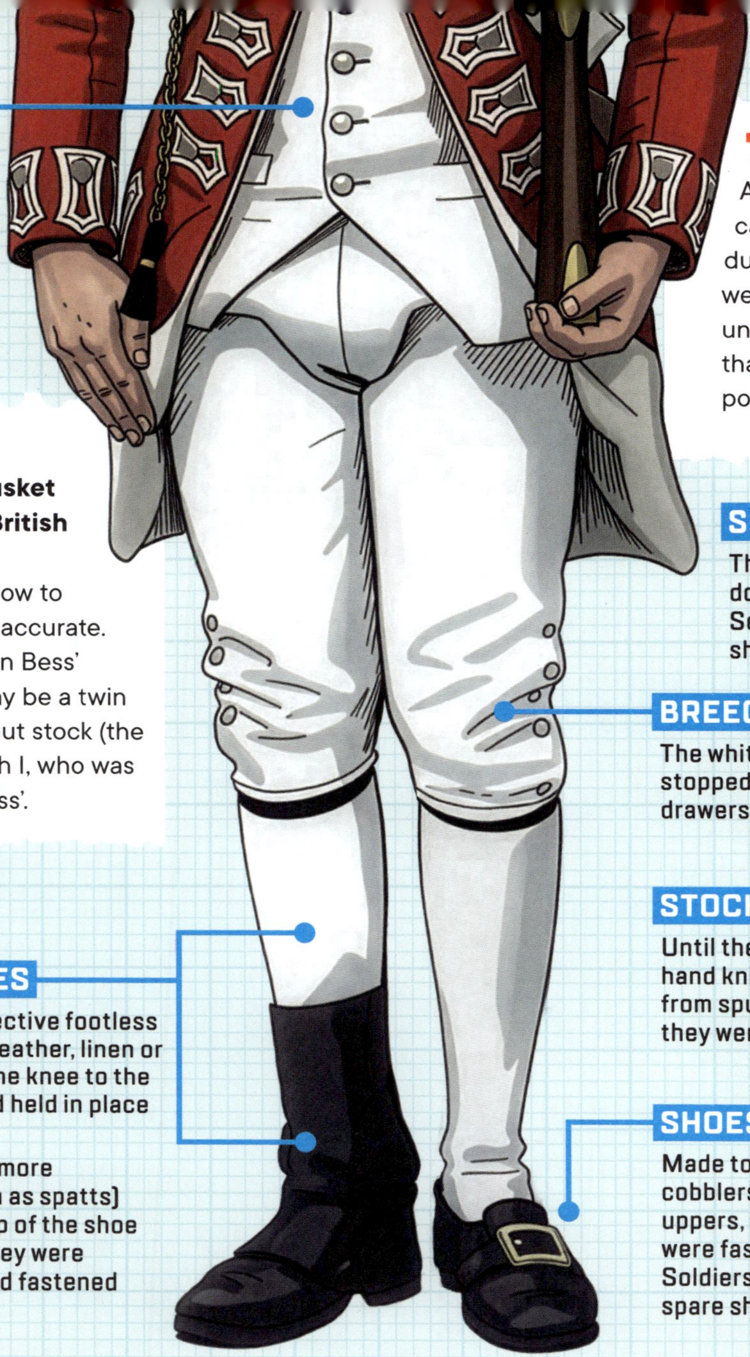

WAISTCOAT

White or buff-coloured and made of broadcloth. To save money, old waistcoat fronts were used to make the back of new waistcoats.

'Brown Bess'

The Short Land Pattern musket was the standard gun for British soldiers at this time.

It fired lead balls but was slow to load, unreliable and not very accurate.

The story behind the 'Brown Bess' nickname is disputed, but may be a twin reference to the gun's walnut stock (the shoulder rest) and Elizabeth I, who was known as 'Good Queen Bess'.

GAITERS & SPATTERDASHES

- **Gaiters** were protective footless socks, made from leather, linen or wool, worn below the knee to the top of the shoe and held in place by straps.
- **Spatterdashes** (more commonly known as spatts) protected the top of the shoe and the ankle. They were made of wool and fastened with buttons.

The forage hat

A red forage or fatigue cap was worn off duty in very cold weather or when undertaking duties that might ruin the posher regimental hat.

SHIRT

Their white linen shirts came down to the soldiers' thighs. Soldiers were issued with four shirts each.

BREECHES

The white broadcloth trousers stopped just below the knee. Linen drawers were worn underneath.

STOCKINGS

Until the late 18th century these were hand knitted from worsted (yarn made from spun wool fibres). From then on, they were spun on a frame.

SHOES

Made to fit by the regiment's cobblers, they had black leather uppers, stiff leather soles and were fastened with a brass buckle. Soldiers were expected to carry spare shoes, soles and heels.

THE CONTINENTAL ARMY

From militias to military force!

When Washington took charge of the 'army of the United Colonies' in 1775 it was a loosely connected network of local militias.

Its soldiers wore their everyday clothing – homespun shirts and britches, leather shoes or moccasins, straw or felt hats, bandanas and beaver hats.

The guns they used on their farms or to hunt were the guns they took to war.

In 1779, Washington ordered that uniforms must be issued. These were made from locally woven cloth or cloth imported from France.

It may not have been up to the high standard of the British, but the uniform brought troops together and distinguished them from the enemy.

TRICORNE HAT

Soldiers wore triangular hats, but some later adopted the French-style 'chapeau de bras' bicorne hat.

BLUE COAT

Chosen to contrast with the British red, they had facings (trim and cuffs) in colours to identify the soldier's home colony.

WHITE WAISTCOATS

Although some wore hunting or rifle shirts (and brown, green or grey versions were sometimes worn over the coat as camouflage).

MILITIA

Some members of the militia bought or were issued with items of uniform.

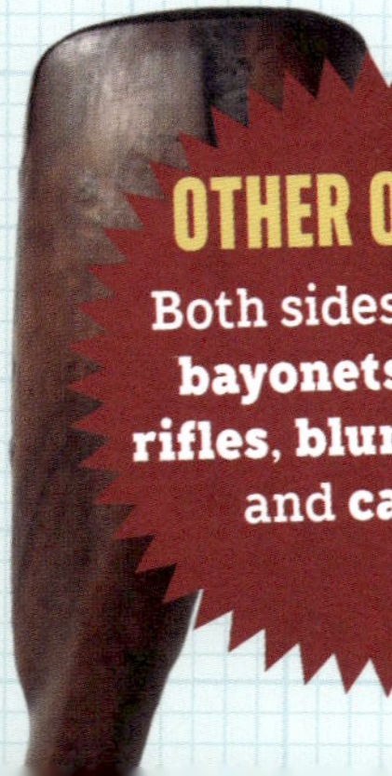

OTHER OPTIONS

Both sides also used **bayonets, pistols, rifles, blunderbusses** and **cannons**

GUNS

COMMITTEE OF SAFETY MUSKET

Made in America and modelled on other guns such as the Brown Bess.

CHARLEVILLE

A musket supplied by the French.

BROWN BESS

British muskets were seized and reused by the Americans.

BREECHES

These were white or beige, and were later replaced by overalls (long trousers).

LEGGINGS OR GAITERS

200,000+

colonists served in the Continental Army during the Revolutionary War. However, it was rare for more than 20,000 to fight at any one time.

AROUND 164,000

people served in local militias

Essential women

It's said a small number of women disguised themselves as men and fought as soldiers.

Female soldiers, such as Deborah Sampson and Margaret Corbin are now famous and celebrated for the contribution they made.

Back home, women sewed, knitted and weaved extra or replacement uniforms. Old clothing and linens were recycled.

Known as 'camp followers', some women travelled with the army to cook, sew and nurse the wounded.

IT'S *COMMON SENSE!*

In January 1776, not all Americans were convinced the best way forward for their colonies was to break with Britain. However, that was before they read a mind-blowing pamphlet written by Englishman **Thomas Paine**...

Common Sense was published on 10 January 1776

In this 46-page pamphlet, Thomas Paine denounced the British monarchy and its empire and argued the case for independence from Britain.

Paine was a talented writer who used simple language, humour, references from the Bible, and memorable phrases to entertain and inform his readers.

Famously, he described America as 'an asylum for human beings', a place for those fleeing the persecution and tyranny of European rulers in the 'old world'.

'THE CAUSE OF AMERICA IS THE CAUSE OF ALL MANKIND'

Paine didn't refer to George III by name, he called him 'the royal brute' instead.

Common Sense sold an estimated 500,000 copies. Paine refused to accept any profit from sales, insisting it was used to fund the printing of more copies.

The pamphlet had a huge influence on colonists' thinking, making popular ideas that would later be included in the Declaration of Independence.

THOMAS PAINE

PAINE'S KILLER QUOTES

'There is something absurd, in supposing a continent to be perpetually governed by an island.'

'O ye that love mankind! Ye that dare oppose, not only the tyranny, but the tyrant, stand forth!'

'Is the power who is jealous of our prosperity, a proper power to govern us?'

'It is the pride of kings which throws mankind into confusion.'

'From the errors of other nations, let us learn wisdom.'

'It is not in numbers, but in unity, that our great strength lies.'

THE INCREDIBLE LIFE OF THOMAS PAINE

1737 Born Thomas Pain on 9 February in Thetford, Norfolk. His Quaker father was a farmer and corset maker.

He was taught basic reading, writing and arithmetic. Aged 13, he followed his father into corsets.

1756 At 19, he went to sea as a privateer on cargo ship, the *Terrible*.

1759 Opened a corset shop in Sandwich, Kent and married Mary Lambert.

The shop went bust and the couple moved to Margate where, tragically, Mary and their baby died in childbirth.

1761 Back in Thetford, Tom became an excise officer (tax collector).

1767 He moved to Cornwall and then briefly to London as a teacher.

1768 Became an excise officer in Lewes, East Sussex.

1771 He married Elizabeth Ollive. After her father's death they took on the family tobacco and grocery business.

1772 He wrote his first political pamphlet. It demanded better pay and working conditions for excise officers. He also debated at the town's Headstrong Club.

1774 Sacked from his job and separated from his wife, he moved to London where he met future Founding Father Benjamin Franklin, who advised him to move to America.

Paine arrived in Philadelphia in November, having almost died of typhoid on

1776 He published *Common Sense* and first of *The American Crisis* series of essay, which inspired Washington and his army to fight on.

1777 Appointed secretary to Congress's Committee for Foreign Affairs.

1779 He was made clerk of the General Assembly of Pennsylvania and started a fund for soldiers with $500 of his own money.

1780 In *Public Good*, he appealed to the colonies to work together as one nation.

1781 Went to France and brought back money, clothing, and ammunition for the revolutionaries.

AFTER THE REVOLUTION

1785 Poverty-stricken, in a petition to Congress endorsed by Washington he asked for their help.

Pennsylvania gave him money and New York gifted him a farm in New Rochelle. There Paine worked on inventions including a new type of iron bridge and a smokeless candle.

1787 Returned to England.

1789 He wrote *Rights of Man*, a defence of the French Revolution. Napoleon claimed he slept with a copy under his pillow.

1792 He was accused of the crime of 'seditious libel' because he supported people's right to overthrow the government.

Paine fled to France. Elected to the French National Convention – despite not being able to speak French! – he helped write the country's constitution.

1793 Arrested and imprisoned amid turmoil in France. While in jail he worked on *The Age of Reason*, which challenged organised religion, and was almost executed for being English!

1802 Returned to the United States.

1809 Died aged 72. Paine is now celebrated as a hero but only six people attended his funeral.

THE DECLARATION OF INDEPENDENCE

WHO WAS THOMAS JEFFERSON?

Born 13 April 1743, in Albemarle County, Virginia.

- Third of 10 children of Jane and Peter, a planter and surveyor.
- Inherited 5,000 acres aged 14.
- Studied Latin, Greek, French, science and law.
- Respected lawyer by the age of 24, elected to Virginia's assembly in 1769.
- Soft-spoken but an exceptional writer. In 1774, he published the popular pamphlet *A Summary View of the Rights of British America*.
- Virginia's Governor from 1779 to 1781.

- Played a vital role in making peace with Britain, the Constitution and the Bill of Rights.
- In 1801, became President of the United States of America.
- Bought Louisiana territory from the French in 1803, doubling the size of the USA.

- Died on 4 July 1826, the 50th anniversary of the Declaration of Independence.

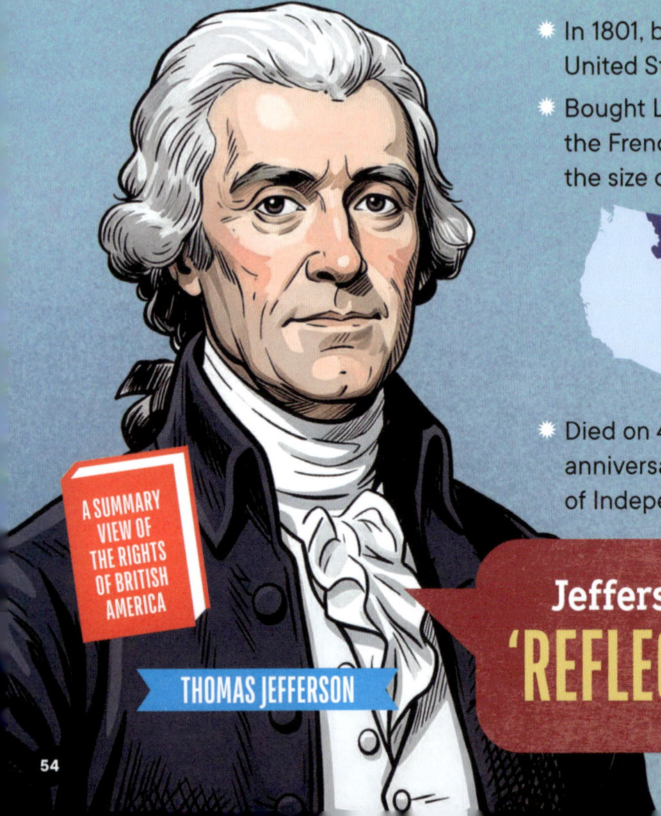

HOW THEY DID IT...

10 MAY

The Second Continental Congress votes on a resolution calling for all colonies to establish their own governments if they have not already done so.

7 JUNE

Virginia delegate Richard Henry Lee presents a resolution in Congress that calls for independence. Congress votes to postpone a vote on independence until July to give delegates a chance to discuss the issue with their colonists.

10 JUNE

Congress appoints the Committee of Five – Thomas Jefferson, John Adams, Benjamin Franklin, Robert R Livingston and Roger Sherman – to write a draft statement of independence for the colonies. The writing is left to Jefferson who, at 33, is the youngest delegate on the committee.

Jefferson said he wanted the declaration to **'REFLECT THE MINDS OF AMERICANS'**

The founding document of the United States of America was approved on 4 July 1776. It announced the separation of the 13 American colonies from their British rulers.

This first draft of the declaration condemned the slave trade that was ***'violating the sacred rights of life and liberty of distant people in Africa'.*** It blamed that trade on the British, but this part was cut out by delegates of the Congress, many of whom were landowners and owned enslaved people.

11 – 28 JUNE

Jefferson writes the first version to which Adams and Franklin make changes.

1 JULY

Delegates reject the Lee Resolution.

2 JULY

A draft declaration presented to Congress. Also, on the second attempt, delegates from 12 colonies vote to approve the Lee Resolution, that states **'...these United Colonies are, and of right ought to be Free and Independent States'**.

Representatives of New York abstained fearing they might soon be invaded by the British.

3 JULY

Congress makes changes to the new draft of the declaration.

4 JULY

The Declaration is adopted by 12 colonies.

5 JULY

Declaration printed, and copies distributed to colonies' assemblies, committees of safety and commanding officers of the Continental Army.

8 JULY

The first public reading of the Declaration takes place in what is now called Independence Square in Philadelphia.

15 JULY

New York delegates approve the Declaration.

19 JULY

Congress 'engrosses' (copies) the Declaration on parchment (treated sheepskin) with a new title, 'The Unanimous Declaration of the Thirteen United States of America' and the members of Congress begin signing it.

'Remember the ladies!'

John Adams was a Founding Father, the United States' first Vice-President and its second President.

Between 1762 and 1801, John and his wife Abigail wrote more than 1,100 letters to each other.

The letters provide insights into major events of the USA's early years. In a now famous letter dated 31 March 1776, Abigail wrote...

'I long to hear that you have declared an independency. And, by the way, in the new code of laws which I suppose it will be necessary for you to make,

I DESIRE YOU WOULD REMEMBER THE LADIES AND BE MORE GENEROUS AND FAVOURABLE TO THEM THAN YOUR ANCESTORS.

Do not put such unlimited power into the hands of the husbands.'

HOWEVER, it would be nearly 150 years before US women were given the right to vote!

IN CONGRESS, JULY 4, 1776.
A DECLARATION
BY THE REPRESENTATIVES OF THE
UNITED STATES OF AMERICA,
IN GENERAL CONGRESS ASSEMBLED.

In CONGRESS, July 4, 1776.

The unanimous Declaration of the thirteen united States of America,

'A John Hancock'

Wealthy Boston merchant John Hancock (remember him from 1768's *Liberty* Affair?), President of the Second Continental Congress, was the first delegate to sign the Declaration of Independence.

In tribute to the spectacular style in which he did that, 'a John Hancock' became American slang for a signature.

INSIDE THE DECLARATION...

With war now raging and its petitions ignored by George III, the Continental Congress's Declaration of Independence put the blame for British misrule on the King and demanded separation from Britain.

Jefferson's impassioned prose, rallied the colonists and united them as a new nation. It also appealed to foreign allies (and the French in particular) for support.

He was inspired by English philosopher John Locke who stated that individuals possessed the right to life, liberty and property.

3 big ideas

1. God made all men equal and gave them certain rights.
2. The main business of government is to protect these rights.
3. If a government fails to do that, the people are free to reject it, revolt and install a new government.

FOUNDING FATHERS

Title given to those delegates who signed the Declaration of Independence. Some historians also include those who later approved the United States' Constitution.

WORD COUNT **1,458**

SIGNATURES **56**

The Declaration's most famous line begins its second paragraph, part of what's known as the preamble...

'WE HOLD THESE TRUTHS TO BE **SELF-EVIDENT**, THAT **ALL MEN ARE CREATED EQUAL**, THAT THEY ARE ENDOWED BY THEIR CREATOR WITH CERTAIN **UNALIENABLE RIGHTS**, THAT AMONG THESE ARE LIFE, LIBERTY AND THE PURSUIT OF HAPPINESS.'

This implies there are no arguments against what follows

That is, created by God without input from a human ruler (e.g. a tyrannical British king!)

These are rights that should not be questioned or taken away

For many Americans this is the most important part of the entire document.

Great Seal of the United States

In the 18th century, every major nation had a seal, a symbol it used on important documents.

After consulting with a committee made up of Benjamin Franklin, John Adams and Thomas Jefferson, Philadelphia artist Pierre Eugène du Simitière came up with a design.

This first attempt incorporated a shield, the motto 'E pluribus unum' (Latin for 'Out of many, one') the 'Eye of Providence in a radiant Triangle' and the year in Roman numerals (MDCCLXXVI).

After many revisions from two more committees, it would be September 1782 before a two-sided seal approved by Congress was used on an official document.

Stars & stripes

On 14 June 1777, Congress adopted the Stars and Stripes as the national flag of the United States.

On this first original flag, 13 red and white stripes represented the 13 colonies and 13 white stars were the new states.

The flag has been changed 26 time since 1777. The current 50-star flag was adopted in 1960.

13-STAR 'BETSY ROSS' FLAG

20 STARS (1818–19)

35 STARS (1863–65)

CURRENT 50-STAR FLAG

The true story of an American icon

CRACKS IN THE LIBERTY BELL

In 1753, a bell was hung in the tower above Philadelphia's Pennsylvania State House...

- Twenty-three years later, this was where the Declaration of Independence was signed. The venue was later renamed Independence Hall.
- The State House Bell was rung to call politicians to meetings and tell the public there was an important announcement to be made.
- It's widely believed that the bell was rung after the Declaration of Independence was approved by congress on 4 July 1776.
- Legend has it that a little blue-eyed boy told his grandfather to ring the bell after he'd heard the Declaration had been agreed.

However...

It was campaigners for the abolition of slavery who gave the bell its name during the 1830s.

It was 71 years later that the 4 July myth was invented as part of *Ring, Grandfather, Ring*, an 1847 story by popular author George Lippard.

There is no evidence that the Liberty Bell was rung on 4 July 1776.

Furthermore, historians say that on 8 July, bells in the city were rung to announce a public reading of the Declaration but the hall's tower was in need of repair so it is unlikely that its bell was rung.

Nonetheless, today the Liberty Bell is central to the story of the American Revolution and the identity of the United States.

INDEPENDENCE HALL

STASHED!

Fearing the British might win the war, colonists hid the bell in a church in Allentown, Pennsylvania for nine months between 1777 and 1778.

'PROCLAIM LIBERTY THROUGHOUT ALL THE LAND UNTO ALL THE INHABITANTS THEREOF'

The inscription on the Liberty Bell

WEIGHS **940KG**

MADE FROM **BRONZE**

(70% copper, 25% tin and small amounts of lead, gold, arsenic, silver and zinc.)

Legacy

When US President Abraham Lincoln died in 1865 his body was brought to Philadelphia to lie in state next to the bell.

Between 1885 and 1915, the Liberty Bell was displayed throughout the United States as a symbol of freedom.

During the 1960s, it was the site of anti-war and civil rights protests.

It was used in campaigns to raise money during World Wars I and II.

The bell was moved from Independence Hall to a nearby glass pavilion in 1976, and then to the Liberty Bell Center in 2003.

It has been featured on coins and stamps and appears on the $100 note.

CRACKS

- In 1751, Isaac Norris, Speaker of the Pennsylvania Assembly, ordered a bell for the tower from London's Whitechapel Foundry. Unfortunately, that bell cracked on the first test ring.
- So, it was melted down and a new one cast. It's said this second bell developed a crack in the early 1840s. In 1846, this crack was deliberately widened in an attempt to stop it from spreading.
- That didn't work. A second crack developed and that meant the bell could no longer be rung. It's been silent ever since.

'A VERY SIGNIFICANT SYMBOL FOR THE ENTIRE DEMOCRATIC WORLD'

NELSON MANDELA

THE WAR CONTINUES...

The Declaration of Independence may have been signed but the Americans still had to beat the British.

Booted out of Boston

Led by its new commander George Washington, the Continental Army forced the British Army to escape the Siege of Boston by sea.

After 11 months of hostilities, around 10,000 British troops boarded 120 ships and sailed out of the port on 17 March 1776.

Washington was awarded the first Congressional Gold Medal for his leadership during the siege. This medal is still awarded today.

German Hessian soldier

THE BATTLE OF LONG ISLAND

The British forces driven out of Boston sailed to Nova Scotia where they waited for reinforcements.

On 3 July 1776, they, along with more troops from home and Hessian soldiers hired from German principalities, landed on Staten Island, New York.

Within a week, 130 British ships were moored just off the island. By mid-August, 32,000 troops were in the area, under the command of General William Howe.

Washington prepared the Continental Army to defend the port of New York on York Island (now Manhattan), knowing its harbour was crucial to the British Navy (led by William's brother, Admiral Richard Howe!). Also, if the British took New York they would have control of the Hudson River and could isolate New England from the rest of the colonies.

Many New Yorkers – merchants and members of the Church of England in particular – remained loyal to Britain.

On 22 August, 4,000 British troops landed on Long Island. Two days later they totalled 20,000... The British attacked American forces on 27 August on the Heights of Guan in Brooklyn. By

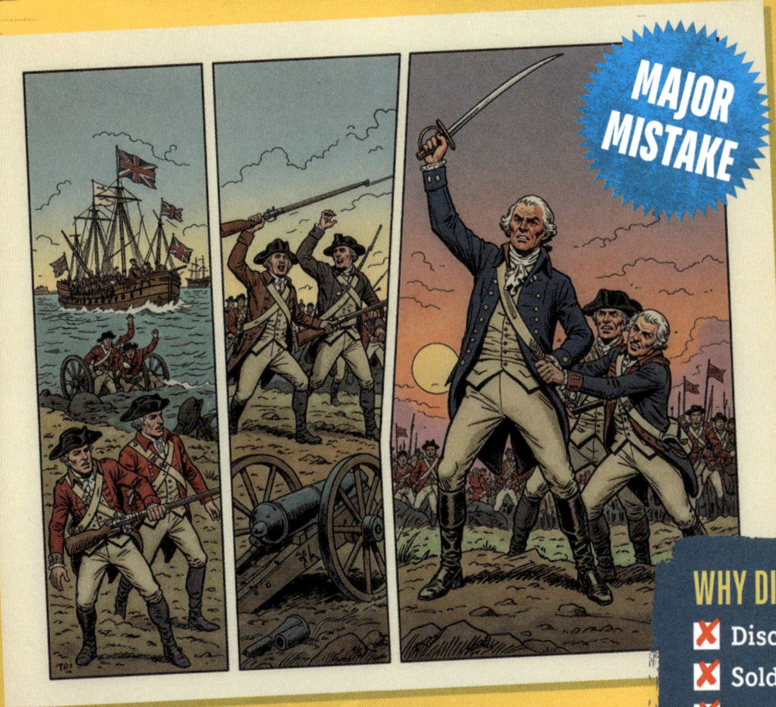

Disaster at Kip's Bay

On 15 September, the British landed in New York at Kip's Bay. The local militia fled when they saw the enemy.

An angry Washington tried and failed to get them to put up a fight and had to be dragged away by his men before he was captured!

The British went on to take the city of New York, which remained under their control until the end of the war.

They also defeated the Americans at White Plains and Fort Washington and in response the Continental Army retreated across New Jersey and into Pennsylvania.

attacking the flank, the British inflicted about 300 losses on the colonists and captured around 1,000 of them.

Although defeated, Washington successfully evacuated his 9,000 troops back to Manhattan Island.

WHY DID WASHINGTON LOSE?

- ✗ Discipline was poor
- ✗ Soldiers from different colonies didn't get along
- ✗ He only had 19,000 troops
- ✗ He split his forces in two – one half stayed to defend Manhattan, the other went to Brooklyn.

ON THE BRITISH SIDE

FOR ✓	AGAINST ✗
Most powerful nation on Earth.	Fighting 3,000 miles away from home.
Largest navy in the world.	Supplies and communication were difficult to organise.
Thousands of trained professional soldiers.	America was huge, wild and probably unconquerable.

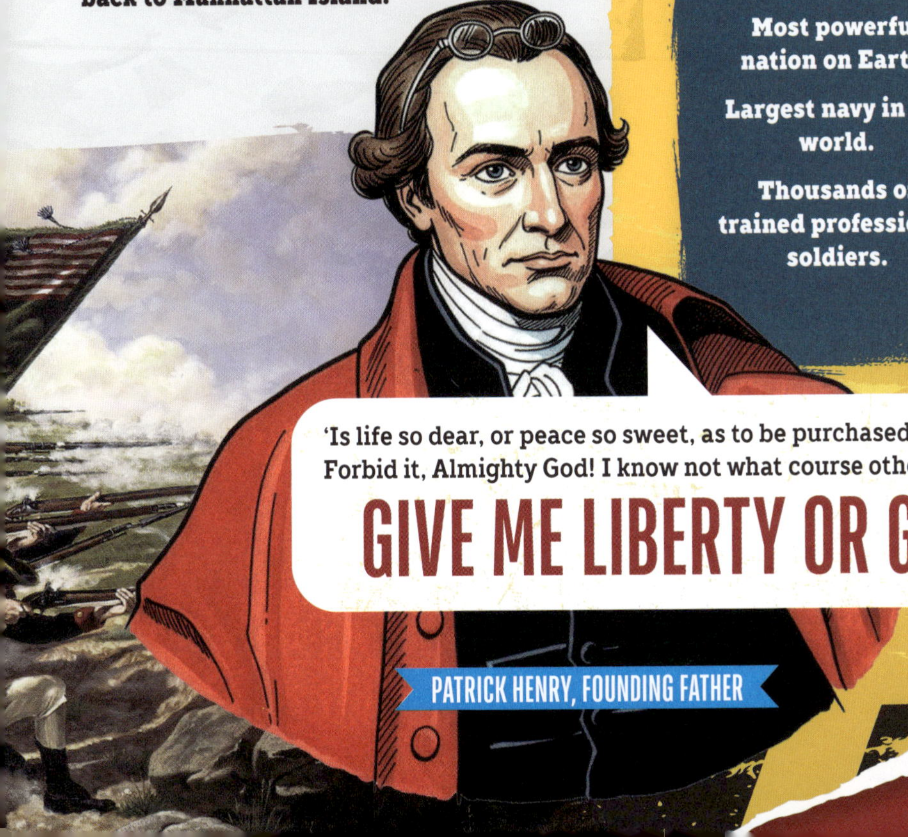

'Is life so dear, or peace so sweet, as to be purchased at the price of chains and slavery? Forbid it, Almighty God! I know not what course others may take; but as for me,

GIVE ME LIBERTY OR GIVE ME DEATH!'

PATRICK HENRY, FOUNDING FATHER

MORE WAR THIS WAY

Crossing the Delaware

At this point, the British looked to have the advantage, but they then made a major mistake....

After taking New York, General Howe had Washington and his army on the run, but rather than chase them down and finish the job, Howe stopped to set up garrisons (military bases).

He hoped the locals would see resistance was useless and commit to the British cause.

This tactic worked in part, as 5,000 colonists pledged allegiance to the crown.

BRITS BACK DOWN

Meanwhile...

Washington and his men were camped out west of the Delaware, the river that divides New Jersey and Pennsylvania.

Morale was low and the troops were weary. What their leader needed was some success on the battlefield that would show all was not lost.

Washington realised that he would always lose all-out battles against his bigger and better resourced enemy. That meant some cunning was needed....

BATTLE OF TRENTON

On the night of Christmas Day 1776, in the middle of a snowstorm, Washington led around 2,400 men across the River Delaware.

After a 10-mile march, in the early hours of the morning they launched a surprise attack on Hessian troops at Trenton.

Within two hours they took the British position without American loss of life.

The Hessians' commander was killed, 1,000 prisoners taken and arms and ammunition were confiscated.

This was a triumph and a turning point in the war, but Washington wasn't finished yet...

BIG MOMENT

ZERO AMERICAN LIVES LOST ONLY 5 WOUNDED

The wounded included 18-year-old James Monroe, who would later become the fifth US President.

JAMES MONROE

BATTLE OF PRINCETON

SURPRISE ATTACK!

The British quickly sent 8,000 troops to Trenton where they skirmished with Washington's forces.

However, during the night, the Continental Army quietly left their camp (leaving fires burning to fool the Redcoats) and marched north to the rear of the Brits' encampment.

At daybreak, Washington attacked three British regiments at Princeton. Around 500 Redcoats were killed as the colonists took more guns and ammunition and then headed north to set up winter camp in Morristown, New Jersey.

Discipline

His troops were often under-fed, under-paid and without uniforms and equipment but Washington kept his army together via strict discipline.

Deserters and thieves were flogged, and it's said Washington had 40 feet-high gallows built *'to hang two or three on it, as an example to others'.*

Nonetheless, many of the soldiers remained loyal to their commander because he demanded more money and supplies for them from Congress.

WHY THESE TWO SMALL VICTORIES WERE IMPORTANT...

- ✓ **Gave heart to the Continental Army**
- ✓ **Inspired a wave of new recruits**
- ✓ **Local militia reclaimed New Jersey**
- ✓ **Supporters abroad saw that the Americans could take on and beat the British.**

MORE BATTLES OVER THE PAGE

RISKY CLASH

BATTLE OF BRANDYWINE

In 1777, British General John Burgoyne led an army from Canada to meet General William Howe's forces marching north from New York.

Their aim was to secure control of the Hudson River and isolate the rowdy rebels of New England.

However, Howe abandoned this plan without telling Burgoyne and instead sailed south to Philadelphia to capture what was, in effect, the colonists' capital.

Washington could not give up the city of his government without a fight. On 11 September, Washington risked a battle with the British at Brandywine Creek, Pennsylvania, knowing his 11,000 were no match for the Redcoats.

The Redcoats attacked from the right and rear and defeated the colonists, but Washington managed to retreat and keep his army intact.

TURNING POINT

BATTLES OF SARATOGA

With Howe in Pennsylvania, the northern part of the Continental Army was able to confront Burgoyne's men at Saratoga, New York on 19 September.

Burgoyne and his 8,000 troops had a terrible time leading up to their defeat. Short of supplies, it's said their baggage train was over three miles long and at times they moved forward less than a mile a day.

Local militia attacked them and blocked their way, and **Burgoyne was forced to build more than 40 new bridges and repair old ones.**

By the time they got to Saratoga, 10,000 patriots were waiting for them. Nonetheless, Burgoyne held off the Americans and gave himself time to wait for reinforcements.

But they never arrived and **a second battle on 7 October ended with the complete surrender of the British** and made a hero of American General Horatio Gates.

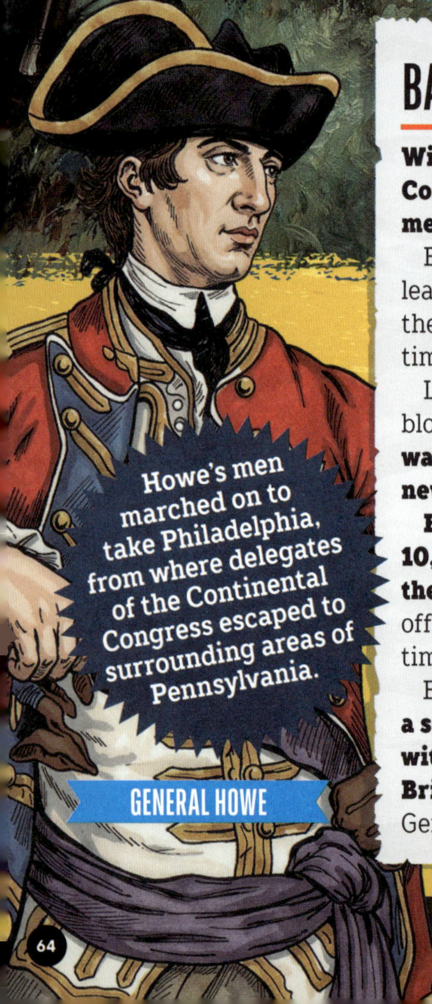

Howe's men marched on to take Philadelphia, from where delegates of the Continental Congress escaped to surrounding areas of Pennsylvania.

GENERAL HOWE

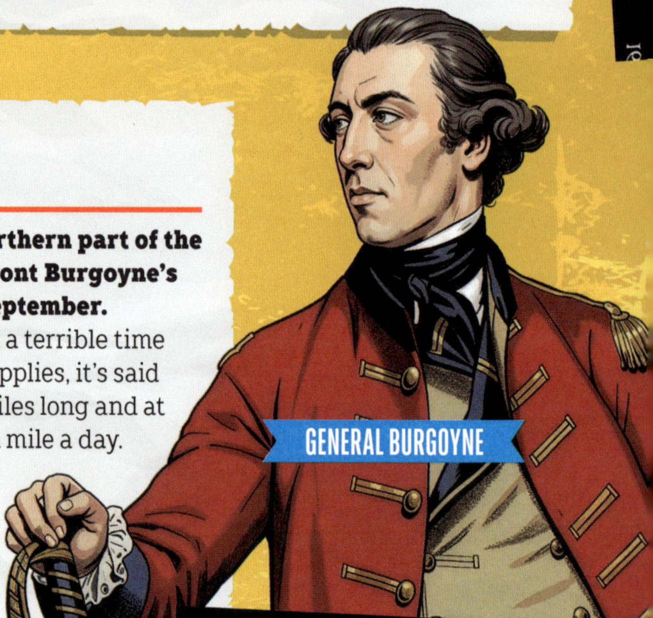

GENERAL BURGOYNE

Saratoga National Historical Park today

An 1898 painting by Howard Pyle of the Continental Army's failed attack at Germantown

NO SURPRISE

BATTLE OF GERMANTOWN

After an unsuccessful surprise attack on British troops at Germantown, Pennsylvania, on 4 October, Washington and his men made camp at Valley Forge, 18 miles outside Philadelphia.

Who's winning really?

- **At this point, the British had control of Philadelphia and New York but had weakened their positions elsewhere.**
- **Washington now saw his best chance of success was smaller but frequent clashes.**
- **As long as he never risked his whole army in one battle, the war would continue, no matter how much territory the British claimed.**

Winter in Valley Forge

With Philadelphia now occupied, in December 1777, Washington led his army to Valley Forge.

A strong strategic position, 18 miles outside the city, this was where 12,000 troops and their followers settled for the winter months.

This army, led by wealthy officers, reflected a country of many different groups, all with their own interests and priorities.

It included untrained civilians, Africans freed from slavery, Native Americans, poor men who had enlisted in the hope of a better life and immigrants from several European countries.

Many different religions were represented, and a large proportion of Washington's men did not speak English.

After the Battle of Brandywine in September, British soldiers had raided supplies and burned down stores and other buildings at Valley Forge.

The Continentals' plan was to regroup and train but because food and medicine were scarce, it's said as many as 2,000 Americans died from disease and exposure.

Washington described *'men without clothes to cover their nakedness, without blankets to lay on, without shoes by which their marches might be traced by the blood from their feet...'*

Despite the problems, the army created a settlement that made Valley Forge the equivalent of the colonies' fourth largest city.

It wasn't until March 1778 that Congress finally gave in to Washington's demands for adequate supplies but **by June, his officers had transformed their troops into a disciplined fighting force.**

2,000 AMERICANS DIED FROM DISEASE & EXPOSURE

VIVE LA FRANCE!

Without Britain's greatest rival, there would be no United States of America. Here's how the French joined the revolution.

SECRET ALLIES

From the beginning of the Revolutionary War, the French had secretly been supplying colonists with guns, ammunition, uniforms and money.

Having lost the Seven Years' War to Britain, France was happy to help an attack on its great rival.

Franklin in Paris

In 1776, Benjamin Franklin became America's unofficial ambassador to France.

After the British surrendered at Saratoga, they offered the colonists a peace deal.

Crafty Franklin used the possibility of a settlement with the Brits to negotiate two treaties with their rivals, the French. And in February 1778, they agreed a trade deal and a military alliance.

This alliance turned a colonial rebellion into a global war as fighting between the British and French broke out in Europe and India soon after.

MULTI-TALENTED BENJAMIN FRANKLIN

DID YOU *know?*

That's awesome, Grandpa! Benjamin's secretary during the negotiations was his 16-year-old grandson William Temple Franklin.

The USA's **$100 bill** is sometimes called a **Benjamin**, a **Benji**, a **Ben** or a **Franklin**, because it features his portrait.

1 PRINTER & PROPRIETOR

Born in Boston in 1706, the young Franklin spent time in London but returned to the colonies in 1726 and became a successful printer. He also founded the influential newspaper the *Pennsylvania Gazette*.

2 POLITICIAN

Early public roles included clerk of the Pennsylvania legislature, postmaster of Philadelphia and organiser of Pennsylvania's militia.

3 INVENTOR

Once he was wealthy enough to retire, Franklin turned to science. With three friends, he conducted groundbreaking experiments with electricity. The most famous involved flying a kite in a thunderstorm. **Among his inventions are the lightning rod, a popular stove and bifocal glasses.**

4 DIPLOMAT

In 1757, Franklin returned to London as a representative of the Pennsylvania Assembly. At first he was loyal to the King. However, he denounced the Stamp Act of 1765 in the British parliament and returned to America in 1775. Elected to the Second Continental Congress, he **helped draft and signed the Declaration of Independence** in 1776 and was sent to France to ask for military aid and diplomatic support.

5 HERO

To the French, Franklin was a hero. His portrait appeared on medallions, snuffboxes and other memorabilia. He used this good will to secure loans and agreements during the war and negotiate peace. In 1785, he went home and **helped write the Constitution**. He died five years later.

6 LEGEND

A self-made man who let nothing hold him back and played a crucial part in the birth of his nation, **Franklin is now seen as an icon of the 'American Dream'.**

'The Hero of the Two Worlds'

The Marquis de Lafayette was born into an aristocratic French family in 1757.

- At 13, he was orphaned and, shortly after made a commissioned officer in the French Army.
- Still in his teens, he travelled to the New World to help in the fight for American independence.
- By 19, he was a major general in the Continental Army. Wounded at the Battle of Brandywine, he later returned to France to demand more resources for the American cause and led troops into battle at Yorktown in 1781.
- Back in the Old World, he was a leading figure in the French Revolution of 1789.
- **Lafayette is known as 'The Hero of the Two Worlds'. Cities, towns and counties across the USA are named after him.**

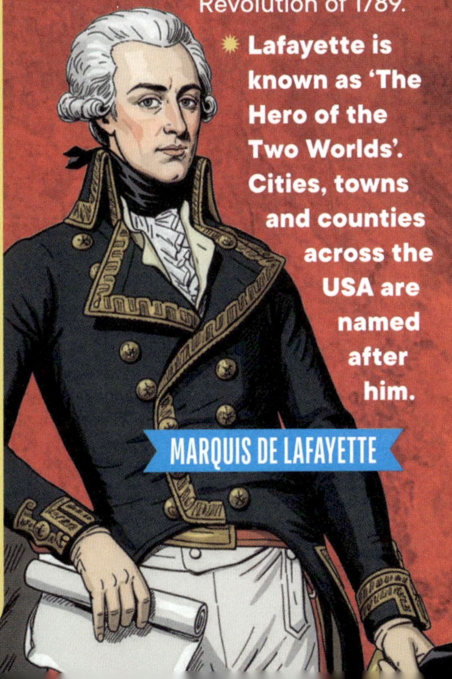

MARQUIS DE LAFAYETTE

SURRENDER!

After the French added their firepower to the colonists' cause, the war began to go America's way.

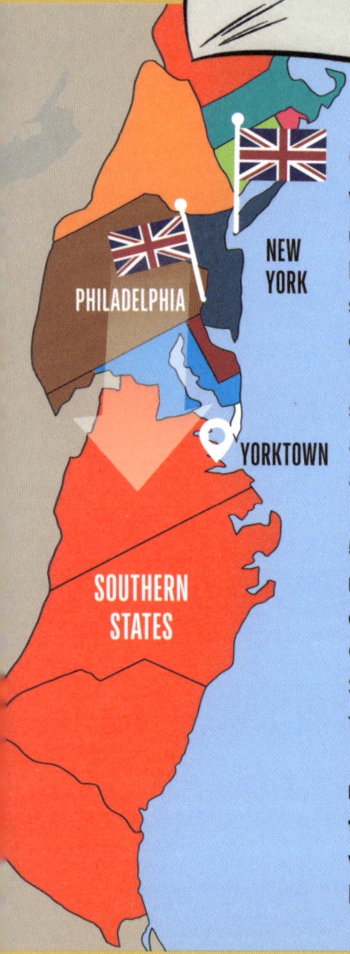

Going South

With New York and Philadelphia under its control, during 1778, the British Army shifted focus to the southern colonies, and protection of its territory in the West Indies.

The Brits believed they had more support among Americans in the South, and throughout Virginia, South Carolina and Georgia they won major gains.

In May 1780 at Charleston, around 5,000 Americans were captured, making it the colonists' greatest defeat of the entire war. In August, General Gates, the American hero of Saratoga, suffered a defeat at Camden that was so bad it ruined his reputation.

However, the British lacked the resources to keep control of these territories. When they withdrew, what was in effect a civil war broke out between local patriots and loyalists.

Washington was furious with General Charles Lee after Lee ordered a retreat

BATTLE OF MONMOUTH

At the end of June 1778, Washington isolated the British by positioning six brigades between the British and the coast of New Jersey.

However, during a clash at Monmouth, the Americans lost their advantage after General Charles Lee ordered his troops to retreat.

Washington tried to intervene, but the chance of a decisive victory was lost, and the British marched on. Lee was arrested, but avoided execution at his trial.

When the French fleet arrived in July 1778, Washington had his troops in New Jersey and New York, and the British in that area were finally confined.

Sea power

With the backing of the French on land and at sea, the Americans took advantage of the new British strategy in the South to put pressure on them elsewhere.

By the spring of 1778, fearing the French Navy would block the Delaware so the colonists could reclaim Philadelphia, the British quickly left the city and retreated to New York.

BATTLE OF YORKTOWN

The final fatal blow was the capture of General Cornwallis, commander of British forces in the South, at Yorktown in Virginia.

French troops first landed in 1780, but by 1781, Congress was considered weak, popular opinion was turning against the war and the French fleet was not providing enough support.

Washington wanted ships to help in fighting the British in the South or their forces in New York.

French Admiral de Grasse said he preferred to attack at Chesapeake, Virginia. So, on August 19, 1781, Washington and soldiers went south, leaving 4,000 men at West Point, New York.

On 14 September, Washington arrived in Williamsburg, Virginia by which time British General Cornwallis and his 7,000 troops had retreated to Yorktown where they were waiting for reinforcements from New York.

Washington and his 5,500 Continentals, 3,500 Virginia militia and 5,000 French soldiers laid siege to the Brits until 19 October when Cornwallis surrendered. (Sort of. He claimed he was too ill to do it and sent someone else instead!) **The conflict dragged on for a few more months but the victory at Yorktown effectively ended the war.**

Storming of Redoubt 10 at Yorktown, a 20th-century painting by H Charles McBarron Jr

Surrender of Lord Cornwallis, an 1820 painting by John Trumbull

25,000
Total number of American **MILITARY CASUALTIES**

Were the British too soft?

Rather than capture territories with brute force, as they had elsewhere, the British generally took a less aggressive, more diplomatic approach in the colonies.

That may have been because most of the colonists were English protestants just like them.

However, it's been suggested that had George III been more of a tyrant he might have won the war...

TRAITOR!

In 1780, Continental Army officer **Benedict Arnold** offered to surrender a fort at West Point to the British in exchange for £20,000.

The plot was discovered and Arnold fled on a British ship. In September 1781, he led Redcoats in a raid on New London, Connecticut. Over 200 years later, to be called a 'Benedict Arnold' in the United States is to be labelled a traitor!

PEACE

The war came to an official end on 3 September 1783 with the signing of the Peace of Paris.

PEACE OF PARIS

The name given to the three separate treaties agreed in 1783 between Britain and the United States, France and Spain.

TREATY OF PARIS

The agreement made between the United States and Britain.

TREATIES OF VERSAILLES

Britain's agreements with France and Spain.

Not necessarily BFFs

Neither Spain nor France wanted the American colonists to be too strong and independent.

In particular, Spain did not want the colonists' success to inspire uprisings in its South American colonies.

FACT THE **BRITS REFUSED TO POSE** FOR THIS PORTRAIT SO IT REMAINS UNFINISHED

Tricky negotiations

Benjamin Franklin, John Adams, John Jay and Henry Laurens represented the Americans in the peace negotiations.

These four Founding Fathers had been told by Congress to consult France during talks, but they ignored that and dealt with the British on their own.

This allowed the Americans to hint at a weakening of their alliance with France and convince the Brits that giving them independence was less of a risk than they might think.

It also meant that the patriots could negotiate boundaries that were less favourable to the French and Spanish.

The Americans then took what had been proposed to France and persuaded them to accept it, telling them that allies should be united when dealing with an enemy. Sneaky!

WHAT WAS AGREED

The United States became an independent country stretching from the Mississippi River in the west, south to the 31st parallel that runs through Louisiana, Mississippi, Alabama and Florida and to the border with British North America (now Canada) in the north.

Britain gave France Senegal in West Africa and the Caribbean island of Tobago.

Fearing that America might ally with Britain, Spain gave up on Gibraltar and settled for the return of Minorca and East and West Florida.

From prison to peace talks

In 1780, Founding Father Henry Laurens was taken prisoner at sea by the British and held in the Tower of London (the only American ever jailed there) for a year. His freedom was exchanged for that of General Cornwallis who the patriots had captured after the surrender at Yorktown.

Washington bows out

On 23 December 1783, George Washington, now widely considered the hero of the revolution, resigned as Commander-in-Chief of the Continental Army.

Washington did not want the new nation to be ruled by military power. He wanted to live in a republic controlled by its citizens, not a dictatorship.

RISE & FALL OF AN EMPIRE

Some historians have said that the Peace of Paris marked the end of the First British Empire that began in the late 17th century.

After losing its American colonies, Britain turned its attention to Asia, Africa and the Pacific.

The empire grew again and was at its largest towards the end of the First World War in 1917, but from then it went into a slow decline.

India's independence in 1947 marked the end of Britain as a major global power and by 1997, when Hong Kong was handed over to China, the empire was finished.

Congress of the United States

CHAPTER 3
WE THE PEOPLE

The Constitution, the Bill of Rights and the Civil War, which laid the foundations for the modern United States of America.

THE UNITED STATES' CONSTITUTION

With the War of Independence won, how the new country was to be run still needed to be agreed.

FAST FACT

A constitution is...
A set of principles, rules and laws that define how a country is governed and the rights of its citizens.

First attempt

In 1777, the Continental Congress adopted The Articles of Confederation. Written by Delaware delegate John Dickinson, this was Congress's first attempt at a constitution.

It was Dickinson who named this confederation of colonies the United States of America.

On 15 November 1777, the Articles of Confederation were adopted by all 13 colonies.

JOHN DICKINSON

In May 1786, **George Washington** wrote that:

'SOMETHING MUST BE DONE, OR THE FABRIC MUST FALL, FOR IT IS CERTAINLY TOTTERING...'

REVOLT AGAINST THE REVOLUTION!

Times were tough for Americans after the war. Among those hardest hit were the men who had served in the Continental Army and the states' militias.

Their pay had been poor and after leaving the army many fell into poverty.

The situation was made worse by merchants who began to demand payment in cash for goods and services.

Once farmers began to lose property to debt collectors, anger in the colonies boiled over...

More unity needed

After the Revolutionary War was won some feared that the United States of America would not last long...

The 13 separate states still had a lot of power and the new country's government struggled to regulate trade and raise taxes.

That meant the national government did not have the money it needed to govern and defend the country from attack.

Also, amid the chaos, the prices of food and goods were going higher and higher...

Daniel Shays knocking over a tax collector

Shays' Rebellion

Continental Army Captain Daniel Shays was among the leaders of a violent uprising against debt collection in Massachusetts in September 1786.

The following January, he led a failed attack on the federal arsenal of weapons at Springfield. In February, after the state's militia defeated Shays and his supporters, he fled to Vermont.

However, what became known as **Shays' Rebellion** achieved its aims. The Massachusetts legislature brought in laws that eased pressure on debtors, and national leaders saw change was needed if the country was to survive.

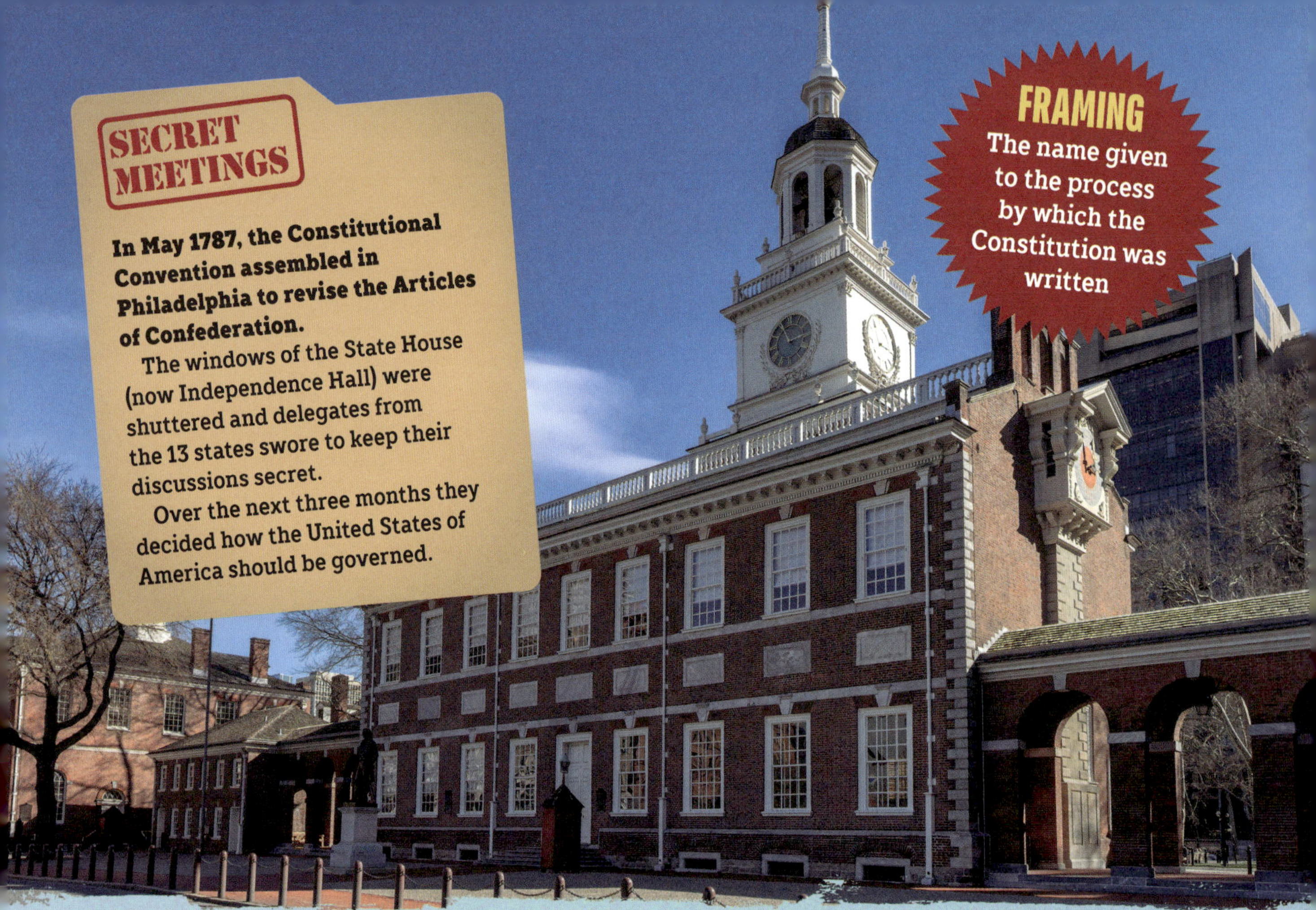

SECRET MEETINGS

In May 1787, the Constitutional Convention assembled in Philadelphia to revise the Articles of Confederation.

The windows of the State House (now Independence Hall) were shuttered and delegates from the 13 states swore to keep their discussions secret.

Over the next three months they decided how the United States of America should be governed.

FRAMING
The name given to the process by which the Constitution was written

HOW SLAVERY SHAPED THE US GOVERNMENT

In the Southern states the slave trade made rich white landowners lots of money.

Southern delegates demanded that slavery should remain legal and that slaves should be counted if it was decided that states with larger populations would have more representatives in government.

Some Northern delegates wanted to abolish slavery and argued that representation should be decided by the size of a state's free population.

In what became known as **The Great Compromise** it was agreed that the country's legislature should have two houses.

- There was to be **THE SENATE** in which all states would be equally represented, and a
- **HOUSE OF REPRESENTATIVES** where the number of a state's representatives was based on the size of its free population plus three-fifths of its enslaved population.

Congress also agreed not to ban the importation of enslaved people until 1808.

3 BRANCHES OF GOVERNMENT

As set out in the Constitution...

EXECUTIVE

President

Members of his/ her Cabinet

LEGISLATIVE

States' representatives in

The Senate

The House of Representatives

JUDICIAL

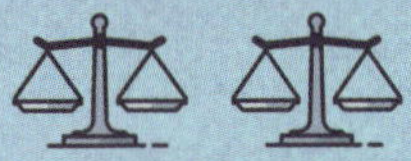

National courts and judges

Headed by Supreme Court

- The system separates powers, so no one branch has total control.
- The three branches are part of a system of checks and balances in which they monitor each other and share power.

Six main goals

1. **'Form a more perfect Union'** for greater cooperation between the states.
2. **'Establish Justice'** in a fair legal system.
3. **'Insure domestic Tranquillity'** by bringing peace and order to the US.
4. **'Provide for the common defence'** to protect the nation.
5. **'Promote the general Welfare'** and help the wellbeing and prosperity of the people.
6. **'Secure the Blessings of Liberty to ourselves and our Posterity'** by protecting Americans' freedom and rights.

Father of the Constitution

At the start of the convention, James Madison put forward his 'Virginia Plan'.

This outlined the structure and ideas behind what, after debates and compromises, became the Constitution. Alongside Madison, war hero Alexander Hamilton and other delegates contributed to the document.

Madison was given the nickname, 'Father of the Constitution' and in 1809 became the fourth president of the United States.

'The First American'

Benjamin Franklin, then 81, was the oldest person to sign the Constitution of the United States. This made him the only man to sign the Declaration of Independence, the Treaty of Paris that made peace with Britain, and the Constitution.

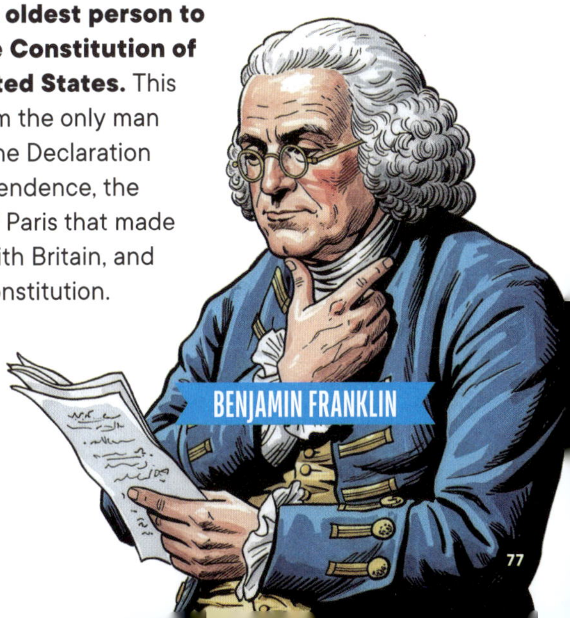

7 ARTICLES OF THE CONSTITUTION

The sections that make up the main text.

ARTICLE 1

The power to impose taxes, borrow money, regulate trade, support military forces and declare war lies with Congress – that is the House of Representatives and the Senate.

- Each state is entitled to two senators who serve terms of six years. Members of the House serve for two years.
- The House can impeach the president (accuse him or her of misconduct). The Senate then judges the case.

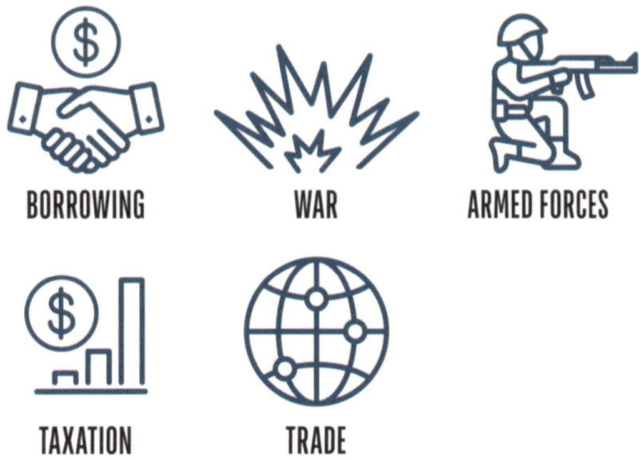

ARTICLE 2

The president of the United States, as selected by the electoral college serves for four years. He or she is the Commander in Chief of the armed forces, can negotiate treaties and grant pardons.

- The president can appoint members of the Cabinet (those in charge of areas of government) and judges but the majority of the Senate must approve these decisions.

ARTICLE 3

The courts have the legal power in the country. They must interpret The Constitution when making decisions.

- As the name suggests, the Supreme Court of the United States is the highest court in the country. It has the power to overrule all other state and federal (national government) courts.

The US Supreme Court

Signed but not sealed...

- The new Constitution was signed by 39 delegates on 17 September 1787.
- It was submitted for ratification (approval) to the 13 states on 28 September.

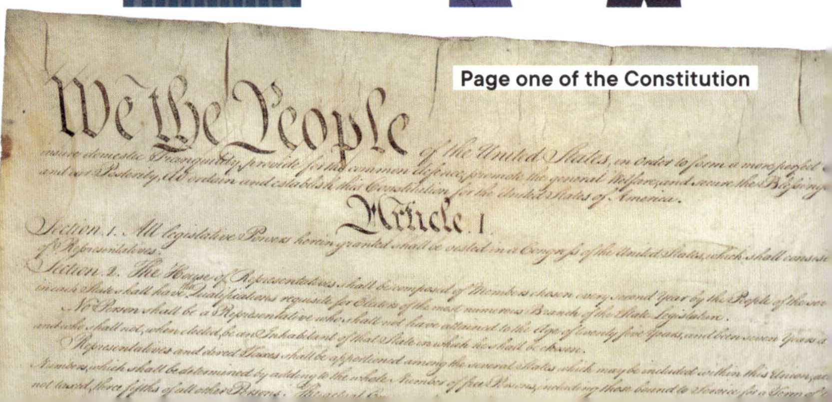

Page one of the Constitution

ARTICLE 4

States must **respect** the official acts and laws of **other states** and have a republican form of government (i.e. have elected rulers).

ARTICLE 5

Amendments to the Constitution can be proposed by a **two-thirds vote** of both houses of Congress and, in special cases, two-thirds of the states.

- They must be ratified by three-quarters of the state legislatures or by conventions in as many states.

ARTICLE 6

The Constitution is 'the **supreme Law** of the Land'.

- All state and federal officials must take an oath to support the Constitution. A person of any religion can take those positions in government.

ARTICLE 7

The **Constitution becomes law** if it is ratified by nine states.

Deal done!

By June 1788, nine states had ratified the Constitution. Congress then chose 4 March 1789 as the date the new government, under the new Constitution, would begin.

States v national government

The Constitution attempted to give the states as much independence as possible.

Only those functions that the states could not handle individually were given to the new national government.

What the Constitution didn't do...

Under the new system, it was left to the states to decide who could vote. They all favoured adult males who owned property.

Women, African Americans and Native Americans were all excluded from voting.

Members of Congress thought men of property had more to lose when making decisions and would therefore be wiser in their judgements. Many of these rich men saw ordinary people as a dangerous unruly mob. **The Constitution describes a system in which people's interests are represented by a select group of people, not a democracy where all adults have a vote.**

The Federalist Papers

These were a series of 85 essays written between 1787 and 1788 by Founding Fathers Alexander Hamilton (of *Hamilton* the musical fame!), James Madison and John Jay.

The essays made the case for the Constitution in an attempt to persuade New York delegates to back the new republican government.

Written under the pen name 'Publius', two centuries later, the essays are still cited in legal cases and political debates.

THE BILL OF RIGHTS

The first 10 changes to the Constitution have been at the centre of life in the United States of America since they were certified in 1791.

Give us our rights!

New Hampshire, the ninth state to ratify the Constitution, did so on condition of a Bill of Rights being adopted.

The other four states – Virginia, New York, North Carolina and Rhode Island – all refused to approve the new form of government without one.

These states wanted the freedom of individual Americans to be protected and restrictions on the powers of government.

THE 10 AMENDMENTS

1ST

Gives citizens the right to **freedom of speech**, a **free press**, freedom of **religious worship** and the right to **peacefully protest** against the government and its decisions.

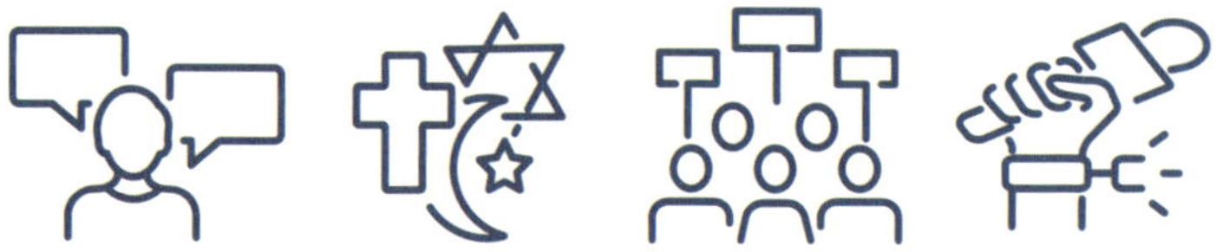

2ND

Protects the right to **keep** and **bear arms**.

3RD

Prevents the government from forcing homeowners to allow soldiers to use their homes.

In September 1789, Congress proposed 12 amendments, 10 of which were ratified by the states. The amendments were certified in December 1791

4TH

Outlaws the unreasonable search and seizure of an individual or their property by the government.

5TH

- States that serious criminal charges must be brought before a grand jury.
- A person cannot be tried twice for the same offence (known as double jeopardy) or have property taken away without being compensated.
- Citizens have the right not to incriminate themselves when giving evidence (this became known as **'pleading the fifth'**).
- A person cannot be imprisoned without due process of law (fair procedures and a trial).

6TH

- Promises the right to a speedy and public trial, to be informed of criminal charges and trial by an impartial jury in criminal cases.
- The accused is allowed to call his or her own witnesses and to be represented by a lawyer.

7TH

Guarantees the right to a jury trial in federal civil cases (non-criminal cases brought by the government).

8TH

Protects against excessive fines, and bail payments, and 'cruel and unusual' punishment.

9TH

Says the inclusion of some rights in the Constitution does not mean people do not have other rights.

10TH

Says the national government only has the powers included in the Constitution. Any other powers belong to the states or to the people.

THE FIRST PRESIDENT

George Washington was the best man for the top job, but he was reluctant to leave his quiet life in the country.

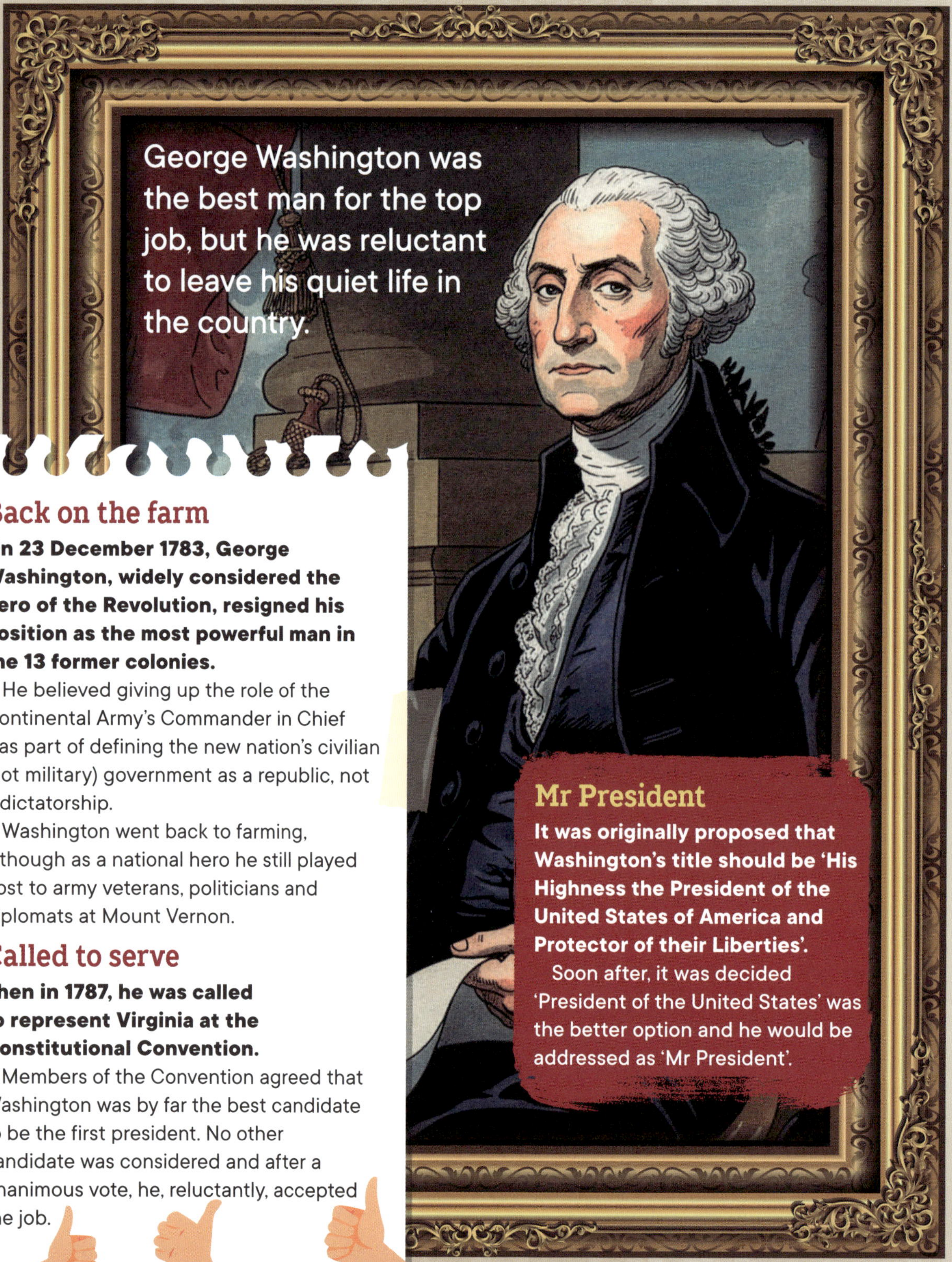

Back on the farm

On 23 December 1783, George Washington, widely considered the hero of the Revolution, resigned his position as the most powerful man in the 13 former colonies.

He believed giving up the role of the Continental Army's Commander in Chief was part of defining the new nation's civilian (not military) government as a republic, not a dictatorship.

Washington went back to farming, although as a national hero he still played host to army veterans, politicians and diplomats at Mount Vernon.

Called to serve

Then in 1787, he was called to represent Virginia at the Constitutional Convention.

Members of the Convention agreed that Washington was by far the best candidate to be the first president. No other candidate was considered and after a unanimous vote, he, reluctantly, accepted the job.

Mr President

It was originally proposed that Washington's title should be 'His Highness the President of the United States of America and Protector of their Liberties'.

Soon after, it was decided 'President of the United States' was the better option and he would be addressed as 'Mr President'.

Triumphant return

In April 1789, Washington travelled from Mount Vernon, Virginia to his inauguration in New York.

People turned out to greet him in villages and towns along the way, and he sailed across the Hudson River into the city in a specially built red, white and blue barge.

A month later, when his wife Martha joined him in Manhattan, guns were fired in salute.

The inauguration of Washington painted by Ramón de Elorriaga around 1898

WHAT HE DID IN OFFICE

- During the eight years he served, Washington tried to **set the tone** for all US presidents to come.
- **Placed himself above other politicians**, opposing the idea of political parties, and stating he was a president for all Americans.
- Established the **First Bank of the United States**, the **United States Mint** and the **United States Customs Service**.

The original US Mint in Philadelphia

- **Remained neutral** when war broke out between France and England in 1793.

- Led troops that put down the **Whiskey Rebellion** (1791 -94) a protest by Pennsylvanian farmers against the first government tax on a US product.
- Reluctantly agreed to **stay on for a second term**.

- **Refused to shake hands**, be paid for the job or agree to a third term.

Political parties

FEDERALISTS supported the Constitution, payment of war and state debts, a central bank, tax laws, trade tariffs, neutrality in foreign wars and peace with Britain.

REPUBLICANS founded by third President Thomas Jefferson and James Madison (both members of Washington's cabinet), they championed equal rights, free trade, freedom of religion and the revolution in France.

Trading names

The Republicans became known as the Democratic Republican Party. That later became what is now the Democratic Party.

The name 'Republican' was taken over in the 1850s by a new party with views close to those of the Federalists and it has had that name ever since.

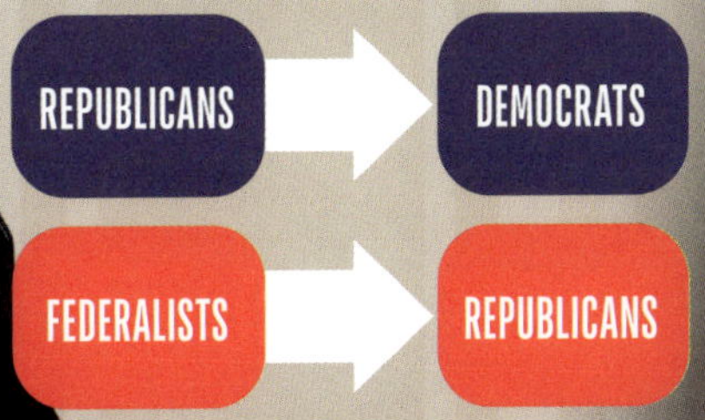

The 1851 painting *Washington as Farmer at Mount Vernon* by Junius Brutus Stearns

SHADOW OF SLAVERY

Few would argue that George Washington was not a great president but doubt surrounds Washington the human being

- As president, Washington lived in the President's House in Philadelphia. **Nine enslaved people** worked there.
- The foundations of the house were rediscovered in 2000. Activists campaigned to have the slaves recognised at the site. Today, their **names are etched in stone** there.
- **Washington did not treat his slaves well**. They were dressed in rags and not given enough food to eat.

- The Pennsylvania Gradual Abolition Act of 1780 stated that after six months in captivity, slaves in that state could petition for their freedom.
  Towards the end of their five months working for him, **Washington would take his slaves out of the state and bring them back, so renewing the six-month term**.
- At the time of his death, there were **over 300 slaves** working on Washington's Virginia plantation.

Retirement

In March 1797 at the age of 65, Washington retired to Mount Vernon.

That was until a brief period in 1798, when he was made Commander in Chief of the army again because war with France looked likely... However, the threat passed and he spent the last two years of his life with family on the farm.

After Washington died at home in bed in December 1799, millions of citizens across the nation mourned his loss.

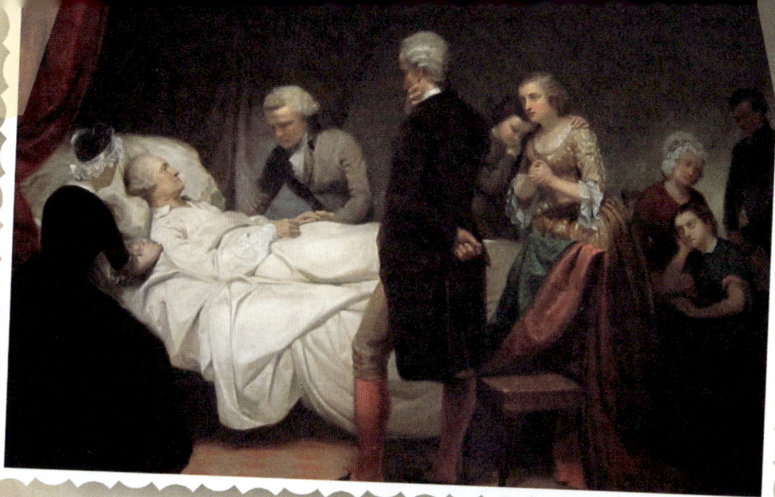

HOW WASHINGTON DC BECAME THE CAPITAL

The Constitution of 1789 called for a 'federal district', separate from any other state, where the United States government would be based.

In 1790, Congress passed the Residence Act that stated that a permanent national capital would be built over an area that took in parts of Virginia and Maryland.

The district's capital city was planned by French architect Pierre Charles L'Enfant and is based on the layout of Paris. It was named in tribute to Washington in 1791.

In 1800, the second president, John Adams, moved into the new city's White House and Congress began meeting in the Capitol Building. Both these buildings were built using slave labour.

The following year, this area was named the District of Columbia and officially became the 'federal district'.

Today, the city is often referred to as DC. It has its own mayor and council, but it is still not a state.

Modern-day Washington DC at night

Mount Rushmore

This 18-metre high 'national memorial' carved into the Black Hills of South Dakota features the heads of four US presidents – George Washington, Thomas Jefferson, Theodore Roosevelt and Abraham Lincoln.

Finished in 1939, it took sculptor Gutzon Borglum 12 years to complete. Borglum named his work 'Shrine of Democracy' and it attracts around two million visitors every year. **The memorial was built on land taken from the Native American Sioux Nation. The Sioux continue to campaign for the return of that land.**

FROM REVOLUTION TO CIVIL WAR

Just 87 years after the Declaration of Independence, the country was once again ripped apart by war.

After Washington

In 1797 John Adams became president. He had been Washington's VP (vice president). Adams tried to remain neutral, but his Alien and Sedition Acts divided the nation. These restricted free speech and allowed foreign-born residents to be deported.

1801

VP Thomas Jefferson became president. Looking to unite the country and remain neutral during the Napoleonic Wars, Jefferson faced serious economic troubles and failed to address the issue of slavery.

1803

The Louisiana Purchase doubled the size of the country, as the US bought territory between the Mississippi River to the Rocky Mountains. It led to the creation of 13 states over an area of 2,144,520 km^2.

1812

War with Britain over naval rights began. The British stormed Washington DC and set fire to the White House in retaliation for America's sacking of York (now Toronto) in Canada. The 1814 Treaty of Ghent peace agreement aimed to abolish the international slave trade.

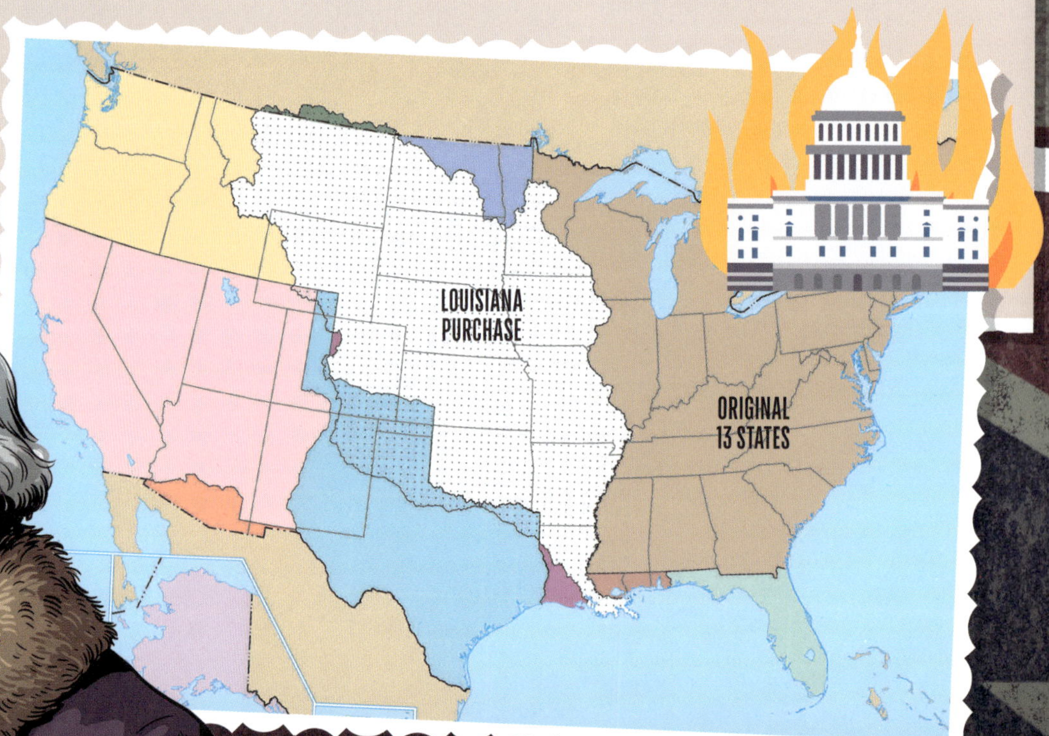

THOMAS JEFFERSON

FACT THE **UNITED STATES DOUBLED** ITS SIZE BY PAYING FRANCE **$15 MILLION** (AROUND $430M OR £324M TODAY). BARGAIN!

North v South

In the decades after the 1812 war, the Union's Northern states embraced the industrial age.

They invested in factories, canals, roads, trains, banking, newspapers and other media.

The Southern states remained dependent on plantations where slave labour was used to grow cotton, tobacco and wheat. Profits were invested in buying more enslaved people.

By 1860, Southern whites' wealth was said to be around twice that of those in the North.

1820 **The Missouri Compromise** allowed Maine into the Union as 'a free state' and Missouri as a 'slave state'.

1830 **The 1830 Indian Removal Act** forced tens of thousands of Native American people to leave their homelands, many of them were moved west on what's now known as the 'Trail of Tears'.

1833 **The Force Bill** allowed the government to enforce federal law in the states.

1848 **The US won the Mexican–American War** and took the land that became California, Arizona and New Mexico. The debate over whether slavery should be employed in these territories divided the North and South.

1850 **Five acts known as 'The Compromise of 1850'** temporarily resolved disputes over slavery.

1854 **The Kansas-Nebraska Act created the two states** and allowed residents to vote on the slavery issue. This led to violent clashes known as 'Bleeding Kansas'.

1857 **The Dred Scott decision** by the Supreme Court ruled that African Americans could not be US citizens and that Congress had no authority to ban slavery.

1860 **Abraham Lincoln was elected president.**

'I HAVE NEVER HAD A FEELING POLITICALLY THAT DID NOT SPRING FROM THE SENTIMENTS EMBODIED IN THE DECLARATION OF INDEPENDENCE.'

ABRAHAM LINCOLN

Born on 12 February 1809 near Hodgenville, Kentucky, Abraham's father Thomas, a poor farmer, was against slavery and moved the family from the slave state of Kentucky to the free state of Indiana.

Abraham's mother died when he was 12 years old. Self-educated, he became a lawyer. Lincoln was the first US president born in a Southern state not to employ enslaved people.

He was known as the **Great Emancipator** and **Honest Abe**.

Lincoln opposed the expansion of slavery, and his election led to **the secession of Southern states**. South Carolina left the Union in December 1860, followed by six other states. They then formed their own government, **the Confederate States of America**.

ABRAHAM LINCOLN

1861 On 12 April, Confederate soldiers attacked the Union's Fort Sumter in South Carolina, and the **American Civil War began...** Within weeks, four more Southern states left the Union to join the Confederacy. In November, the Mexican-American War hero Jefferson Davis was elected the Confederacy's President.

Bombardment of Fort Sumter

1862 Lincoln promised freedom for enslaved people in any Confederate state that did not return to the Union by the end of the year.

1863 On 1 January, Lincoln signed the **Emancipation Proclamation** that freed the three million slaves in the Southern states. In November, he delivered the **Gettysburg Address** at a site in Pennsylvania where a civil war battle had taken place four months earlier.

In what is now one of the most famous speeches in US history, Lincoln vowed that...

'GOVERNMENT OF THE PEOPLE, BY THE PEOPLE, FOR THE PEOPLE SHALL NOT PERISH FROM THE EARTH.'

ABRAHAM LINCOLN

JEFFERSON DAVIS
Confederate President

'IF SLAVERY IS NOT WRONG, NOTHING IS WRONG.'

ABRAHAM LINCOLN

1864

Lincoln was re-elected as president in November.

Five months later, **on 9 April 1865, General Robert E Lee of the Confederate States Army, surrendered** to the Union's General Ulysses S Grant at Appomattox Court House in Virginia.

Death of a hero

On the night of 14 April 1865, John Wilkes Booth, a famous actor and a supporter of the Confederacy, assassinated Lincoln while he watched a performance of the comedy *Our American Cousin* at Ford's Theatre, Washington DC.

The 13th Amendment

Ratified on 6 December 1865, this change to the Constitution abolished slavery.

4

The number of US **presidents** that have been **assassinated** while in office. The others are James A Garfield (1881), William McKinley (1901) and John F Kennedy (1963).

851,000

The estimated number of **soldiers killed** during the US Civil War (around 2% of the population in 1860).

271

The word count for the **Gettysburg Address.** It begins with a reference to the Declaration of Independence.

AROUND 200,000

The number of Black men, many of them freed slaves, who fought for the Union.

Juneteenth

Celebrated on 19 June since 1866, this annual national holiday commemorates the end of slavery in the United States. It marks the date in 1865 when an estimated 250,000 slaves in Texas were freed.

THE FIGHT GOES ON

The United States was reunited and slavery made illegal, but many more issues were still to be resolved...

The 1867 engraving *Freedmen Voting in New Orleans* by Frank Leslie

Reconstruction

In the period after the Civil War known as the Reconstruction, Congress attempted to address issues post-slavery and bring the 11 Southern states back into the Union.

Democracy in America

The word 'democracy' does not appear anywhere in the US Constitution.

Less than 1.8% of the United States population voted when George Washington was elected the first president in 1789.

Voting was limited to property-owning white males over the age of 21.

The electorate was expanded over time but because the 10th Amendment had left the decision on who could vote to individual states, progress was slow.

Some states had laws that meant only those who paid taxes or passed literacy tests were allowed to vote. These laws often excluded minorities.

FACT **DEMOCRACY** IS A SYSTEM OF GOVERNMENT IN WHICH THE **PEOPLE OF A COUNTRY VOTE** TO ELECT THEIR REPRESENTATIVES

THE BLACK VOTE

The 14th Amendment adopted in 1868 granted citizenship and equal civil and legal rights to 'all persons born or naturalised in the United States' including African Americans and those freed from slavery.

✱ The 15th Amendment of 1870 guaranteed that the right to vote could not be denied based on 'race, color or previous condition of servitude.'

The Civil Rights Act of 1875 outlawed racial discrimination in hotels, restaurants, theatres and on railways.

✱ However, the US Supreme Court's Civil Rights Cases (1883) stopped Congress from taking action against violations of African Americans' rights by individuals, organisations and businesses.

✱ Between 1887 and 1892, nine Southern states brought in laws requiring separation according to race on public transport. These were examples of what became known as the discriminatory 'Jim Crow laws'.

✱ In 1909, the National Association for the Advancement of Colored People (NAACP) was formed. The NAACP campaigned to abolish all forms of discrimination including that in housing, education, employment and voting.

MARTIN LUTHER KING

SUFFRAGE The right to vote in political elections

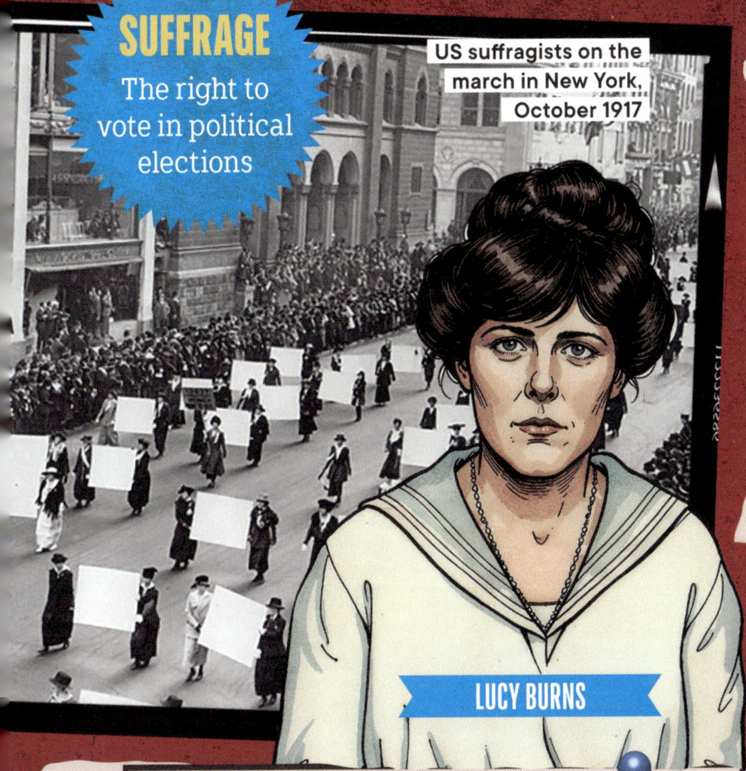
US suffragists on the march in New York, October 1917

LUCY BURNS

NATIVE AMERICANS' RIGHTS

The 10th amendment was among several obstacles to progress for the United States' Indigenous Peoples. Many states were reluctant to grant them rights, including the vote.

- Just under half of their populations were given citizenship and the right to vote by the 1924 Indian Rights Act.
- It would not be until 1965's Federal Voting Rights Act overruled state-level laws that Native Americans were granted their full rights as citizens.

Chiefs of the Native American Sioux tribe photographed in 1899

WOMEN'S SUFFRAGE

In July 1848, the Seneca Falls Convention, held in Seneca Falls, New York, launched the women's rights movement and called for women's suffrage.

- During the second half of the 19th century, some states extended voting rights to women but what was needed was a new law at national level.
- A constitutional amendment was first introduced in 1878, and, by 1918, 15 states allowed women to vote.
- Pressure from the National Woman's Party finally brought about women's suffrage.
- In 1917, the party's leaders **Alice Paul and Lucy Burns** were among the hundreds of protesters outside the White House.
- A typical banner read: *'Twenty million women are denied the right to vote. The president is the chief opponent of their enfranchisement.'*
- Three years later women were given the right to vote via the 19th Amendment.

Meanwhile, elsewhere in the world...

The American Revolution inspired uprisings among other oppressed people...

FRANCE 1789 The overthrow of King Louis XVI and the Ancien Régime ('old order') was inspired by the success of the American Revolution and many of the writers (including Thomas Paine) and ideas that had motivated the Founding Fathers.

HAITI 1791 Haiti became an independent nation after a series of clashes with its British and French colonisers. In 1804, it became the first country to be founded by previously enslaved people.

LATIN AMERICA 1808–26 After conflicts with their Spanish rulers, Mexico, Gran Colombia (now Venezuela, Colombia and Ecuador), Peru, Bolivia, Chile and Argentina all won their independence. Also, Brazil broke away from Portugal in 1822.

USA TODAY

How the US government, as set out in the Constitution, works now...

LEGISLATIVE BRANCH

Inside the House of Representatives

Congress

- **This is made up of two sets of elected politicians – the Senate and the House of Representatives.**
- The two chambers must agree on a bill before it can be signed by the president and made law.
- Both meet in the Capitol Building.

THE SENATE

- **There are two senators from each state – so 100 in total.**
- Senators are voted for by people in their state, and they serve a six-year term.

HOUSE OF REPRESENTATIVES

- **435 representatives (congressmen and congresswomen).**
- Each state has a different number of representatives: states with more people have more representatives.
- Representatives are elected every two years.
- The speaker of the House is its leader, and is elected by the other representatives.
- Mr or Madam Speaker is second in the line of succession to the presidency (after the vice president).

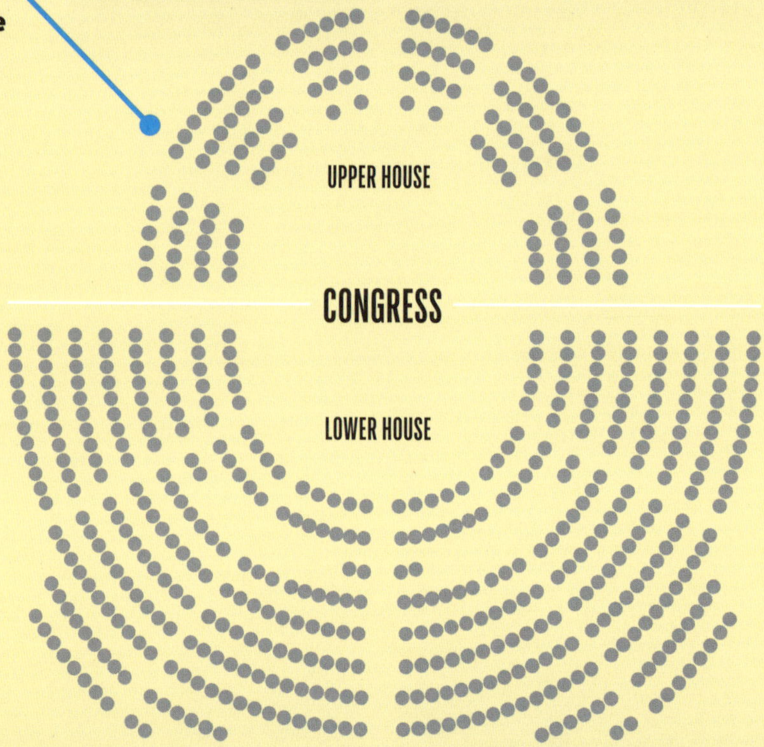

USA POPULATION

1775
2.5 MILLION
(includes around 460,000 enslaved people & excludes Native Americans)

2025
342 MILLION
(4% of the world's population)

EXECUTIVE BRANCH

President & cabinet

- **The president and his Cabinet make up the executive branch.**
- This has 15 different departments which oversee major areas of American life such as the economy, education, defence and agriculture.
- The president chooses the vice president and who will be head of each department and together they make up the cabinet, but the Senate has to approve all his appointments.

JUDICIAL BRANCH

Courts & judges

- **The Unites States courts decide on the meaning of laws, how they work in real-life situations, and whether a law is in line with the rules of the Constitution.**
- The Supreme Court has the power to overturn any US law (either federal or state).
- It has nine judges all appointed by the president and approved by the Senate.
- The judges are called 'justices' and their leader is the 'chief justice'.
- These justices have their jobs for life.
- They can only be removed if they are found to have committed a crime.

The US Supreme Court justices photographed in June 2022

Who does what

STATE GOVERNMENT

- **Public health & safety**
- **Police & fire departments**
- **Roads**
- **Schools**
- **Trade inside the state**

FEDERAL GOVERNMENT

- **Diplomacy**
- **Overseas trade**
- **War**

SHARED RESPONSIBILITIES

- **Making & enforcing laws**
- **Taxes**

Democrats v Republicans

DEMOCRATS

REPUBLICANS

There are two main political parties in the USA – Democrats and Republicans. Because they are so powerful, the US government is sometimes called a 'two-party system'.

TWO IS ENOUGH!

The 22nd Amendment of 1951 **prohibits anyone being president more than twice**

The president must be...

- ✔ At least 35 years old
- ✔ A natural born US citizen
- ✔ A resident of the US for at least 14 years

Presidential election

- Every four years a general election is held.
- In line with Article II of the Constitution, voters elect 538 members (ordinary people chosen by political parties in each state) of the electoral college.
- The electoral college then elects the president and vice president.

Impeachment

The Constitution states the president can be impeached and removed from office for a number of offences. These include 'Treason, Bribery or other high Crimes and Misdemeanors'. Impeachment is the process by which charges can be brought against the president. A majority in the House of Representatives must vote in favour of impeachment for the process to begin.

FACT JUST **THREE PRESIDENTS** HAVE BEEN **IMPEACHED**. THEY ARE **ANDREW JOHNSON**, **BILL CLINTON** AND **DONALD TRUMP**.

GLOSSARY

BROWN BESS
Nickname for the Short Land Pattern musket used by both sides during American Revolutionary War.

CABINET
In politics, a group of people who advise and help the president govern the country. Otherwise, a handy item of furniture used for storage.

CAPITOL
Government building in the United States.

CIVIL WAR
A war fought between groups within the same country.

COLONY
A territory controlled by a distant, more powerful country.

CONFEDERATION
A group of states or organisations that comes together in a common cause.

CONGRESS
A meeting of representatives for debate and law-making. Also, the name given to the USA's two chambers of elected representatives.

CONSTITUTION
A set of principles, rules and laws that define how a country is governed and the rights of its citizens.

DEMOCRACY
A system of government in which the people of a country can vote to elect their representatives.

FOUNDING FATHERS
Men that contributed to and signed the Declaration of Independence.

GAITERS
Protective footless socks made from leather linen or wool.

HESSIANS
German soldiers hired by the British to fight the colonists.

HOUSE OF REPRESENTATIVES
One of two chambers of elected representatives of United States' people.

INDEPENDENT
To be free from the control of others.

LEGISLATURE
A groupof people with the power to make laws.

LIBERTY
The state of being free to act, speak, and live as you please.

MILITIA
A military force made up of ordinary people, not professional soldiers.

MONARCHY
A government ruled by an unelected king or queen.

PAMPHLET
A small booklet or leaflet on one subject.

PATRIOT
A person who loves and defends their country.

PRESIDENT
The elected head of a republic.

REDCOAT
The nickname for 18th-century British soldiers.

REPUBLIC
A country where power is held by the people and their representatives.

REVOLUTION
The overthrow of a government and the installation of a new system.

RIGHT
A moral or legal entitlement.

SENATE
One of two chambers of elected representatives of United States' people.

SPATTERDASHES
Commonly known as 'spatts'. Protectors of the top of the shoe and ankle.

SUFFRAGE
The right to vote in political elections.

TARIFF
A tax paid on imported goods.

TERM
A fixed period of time.

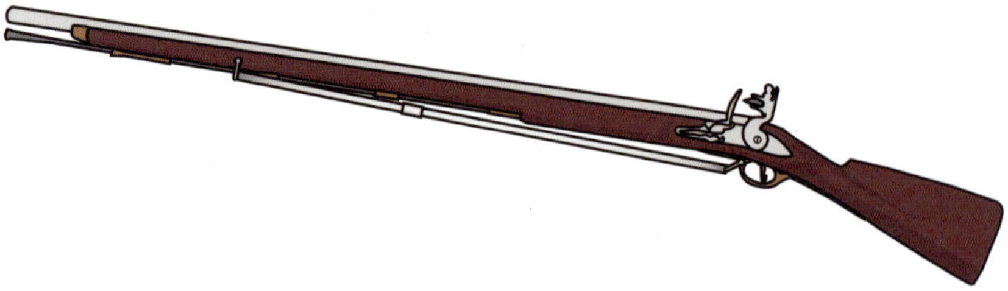

INDEX

First published 2026 by Button Books, an imprint of Guild of Master Craftsman Publications Ltd, Castle Place, 166 High Street, Lewes, East Sussex, BN7 1XU, UK (www.buttonbooks.co.uk). Copyright in the Work © GMC Publications Ltd, 2026. ISBN 9781787081925. Distributed by Publishers Group West in the United States. All rights reserved. No part of this publication may be reproduced, stored in a retrieval system, or transmitted in any form or by any means without the prior permission of the publisher and copyright owner. While every effort has been made to obtain permission from the copyright holders for all material used in this book, the publishers will be pleased to hear from anyone who has not been appropriately acknowledged and to make the correction in future reprints. The publishers and authors can accept no legal responsibility for any consequences arising from the application of information, advice, or instructions given in this publication. The EEA authorised representative is Authorised Rep Compliance Ltd., Ground Floor, 71 Baggot Street Lower, Dublin, DO2 P593, Ireland (www.arccompliance.com). A catalogue record for this book is available from the British Library. Words: Robert Hiley Design: Tim Lambert Editorial: Jonathan Harwood, Jane Roe, Anne Guillot Publisher: Jonathan Grogan. Production: Jim Bulley. Photos/illustrations: Michelle Urra, Alex Bailey, Shutterstock.com. Colour origination by GMC Reprographics. Printed and bound in China.

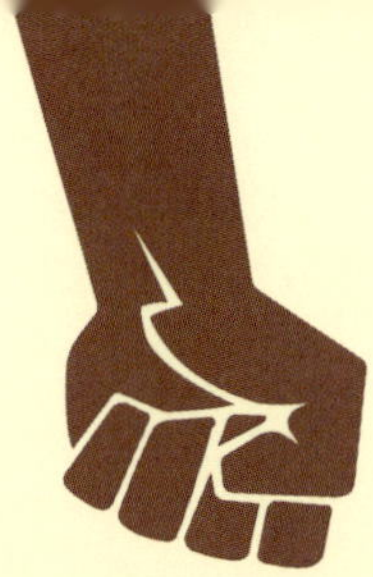

SESQUICENTENNIAL EXPOSITION
1776
UNITED STATES POSTAGE
1926
2
TWO CENTS
2

PHILLY

Daily Post
NO, TO BRITISH RULES IN THE COLONIES!

CHARLESTON

MY COLONY IS MY COUNTRY!
NEW YORK
STATE
U.S.
of the STAMP
An Emblem of the Effects
O! the fatal Stamp
NO TAXATION WITHOUT REPRESENTATION!
BOSTON
TEA
PARTY